MODERN BUILDING

MODERN BUILDING

ITS NATURE, PROBLEMS, AND FORMS

BY WALTER CURT BEHRENDT

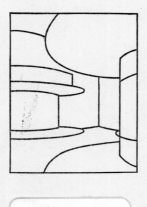

HARCOURT, BRACE AND COMPANY, NEW YORK

Designed by Robert Josephy

PRINTED IN THE UNITED STATES OF AMERICA

PREFACE

Modern building was long an inspiration before it became a reality. For almost a century the idea of developing a new style adapted to the needs of a new age, was carried on by a spiritual movement of international scope whose strength and perseverance finally succeeded in the realization of new forms of building.

Rather than a history of modern architecture complete as to names and biographical data, this book is an essay on the spirit of modern building, its origins, problems, and forms. A brief selection of historical books, already existing by the hundreds and offering valuable sources of information, is to be found in the bibliography. The author has gratefully made use of them, to his own benefit; and so may the reader of this essay; an essay intended to trace the rise and development of ideas that determined modern building and prepared the advent of a new style.

WALTER CURT BEHRENDT

Hanover, N. H.
Dartmouth College

ACKNOWLEDGMENT

This book could not have been written without the help of my American friends.

There were, first of all, Charles and Gene Whitaker who stretched out their hands helping me to find my way into this country and to make a new start in life. In the beginning of 1934, some preliminary work for this book was done in their home, with Charles Whitaker as an inspiring critic and sensitive translator.

Then it was Lewis Mumford who initiated and, with the aid of Clarence S. Stein, arranged for a series of public lectures on modern building which was given at Dartmouth College in winter 1934-35. In preparing these lectures I enjoyed the genuine co-operation of the Department of Art and the aid and advice of its members, particularly of Artemas Packard and C. P. Lathrop. Hugh and Betty Morrison were constantly helpful in revising my notes.

These lectures form the nucleus of this book. In an act of self-sacrifice, proving his friendship as well as his passion as a teacher, Sidney Cox aided me in revising the manuscript, transforming into readable English what represented the first attempt on the author's part to write a book in another than his mother tongue.

Let it be added that the principal ideas of this book which for many years have occupied my mind have been cleared and elaborated in many discussions with my German architect friends, among whom Hugo Häring with his *Philosophy of Forms* (not yet published) has given me the strongest impetus.

For courtesies in allowing pictures to be reproduced, I am indebted to Henry Russell Hitchcock; Catherine Bauer; Compagnie Aérienne Française; Department of Architecture, The Museum of Modern Art, New York; School of Architecture Library, Harvard University; The Architectural Review, London; Swedish Travel Information Bureau; Preussische Hochbauverwaltung, Berlin; *Country Life, Ltd.;* Aero Service Corporation; World Wide Photos; Chicago Architectural Photographing Company, and Keystone-Underwood.

I feel very grateful to my friends and to all those who helped me in accomplishing this work.

WALTER CURT BEHRENDT

CONTENTS

ILLUSTRATIONS

MODERN BUILDING

INTRODUCTION: THE PROBLEM OF ORDER

In 1770, a young student from Frankfort set out to enter the University of Strasbourg, where his father wanted him to study law. Soon after his arrival in the foreign town, he went to see the famous cathedral, and from his very first moment in the presence of this masterpiece of the Gothic he was deeply impressed.

His previous studies in art had been guided by his father, who had taught him, in accordance with the esthetic ideals of his time, to regard the works of the ancients as the height of taste and the measure of beauty. In his father's house, every day he had seen a series of Roman views, with which the Imperial Councilor Johann Kaspar Goethe had adorned the ante-room: engravings by some of the accomplished predecessors of Piranesi, views of the Piazza del Popolo, the Colosseum, St. Peter's Church, within and without, and the Piazza of St. Peter's. In *Dichtung und Wahrheit,* we are told how these images impressed themselves deeply upon the youngster, trained his eyes, formed and determined his judgment in art.

From those examples, when he first approached the Strasbourg Cathedral, his head was full, as he said, of a general knowledge of good taste. From hearsay he knew about harmony of masses and clearness of forms; and by esthetic doctrine he was a pro-

3

fessed adversary of Gothic jig-saw work. Gothic he had been taught to interpret as something barbarous. But now, upon beholding the great cathedral, his learned doctrine was overthrown by immediate experience. And trusting the deep impression, he cast aside the traditional prejudices of his time. He had perceived the greatness and sublimity of Gothic art.

From intuitive perception he then proceeded to study and investigation. A spirit always striving to order isolated experiences, he reflected on his impression. His findings were given form and published in his famous essay *Von deutscher Baukunst,* dedicated to Erwin von Steinbach, the builder of the Cathedral. In its clear conception of general principles, the paper reveals the divination of a genius. In language poetic with the passion and enthusiasm of youth, the author praised the originality of the Gothic building, which seemed to him "not a product of human hands, but a creation of nature, everything perfect in form, even to the smallest detail, everything subordinated to the whole." In his imagination he set the Cathedral face to face with the remembered models of classicism. Their polished beauty seemed to him the mere result of esthetic rules, while the naturalness and even harshness of the Gothic building seemed to manifest creative power. Interpreting his experience, he came to say: "Art is formative long before it is fine, and yet is true and great, indeed, often truer and greater than fine art itself."

THE DUALISM OF THE CREATIVE INSTINCT

We set out from this profound statement because it refers to a prime phenomenon of the creative instinct and leads us right into the problem of order, which is the core of our discussion.

Formative art and fine art: in this antithesis there are traced and formulated two potentialities to be found in Western art. To be sure, this distinction is not meant to be a criticism of the results of artistic production, or a judgment comparing their esthetic values. Both the opposing potentialities are immanent in man's creative instinct. Formative art and fine art: this antithesis differentiates two kinds of art produced by the creative instinct, the manifestations of which share in that inherent antagonism between nature and reason, sense and thought, which has determined the culture of Western mankind ever since Socrates the philosopher proclaimed in the agora at Athens the supreme function of the *Nous,* that is to say *Reason*. According to that antagonism, human creative instinct is to be seen moving between two poles, manifesting itself in two different ways, which may be distinguished as intuitive and constructive imagination. With these terms there are characterized two elemental impulses that grow out of a common root, but separate into two opposing directions, and acting in individuals, lead to two different kinds of form.

This dualism of creative instinct, based upon the everlasting antagonism of sense and thought, involves two different attitudes towards the cosmos. The work of the artist is always based upon the intuition he has of the world. In his attitude to the cosmos, the artist may see and feel the world as a finite or infinite reality. He may take reality as it appears in its overflowing exuberance and variety of individual life. His attitude is close to nature, filled with awe and respect for the manifoldness of her mani-

5

festations. Following this attitude, not yet wrested from simplicity, he will then produce forms of an individual character, existing but once and not repeated. Guided by intuitive imagination, faithfully devoted to the given object, this simple state of creative instinct produces what Goethe called "formative art."

There is, on the other hand, an attitude which feels puzzled by reality, upset by the overwhelming exuberance of individual life, entangled by the multitude and variety of its appearance. The artist tending toward such an attitude, will look for the unchangeable in the changing, for the continuous in the spasmodic shifting of things, for the everlasting in the temporal, in short for an ultimate law bringing order to the chaos of appearances. Subjecting the world to that law, which is the product of his own mind, he makes this law and its fixed principles the starting point in creating his forms. Reducing the infinite detail of appearances to a certain system of norms and lasting measures, he aims at forms of an idealized type, at forms representing an image of highest perfection, an ideal of beauty itself. From such a refined state of creative instinct came into being what Goethe called "fine art."

Intuitive imagination and constructive imagination, true devotion to life in its individual aspects on the one hand, and intense desire for the absolute, for the general law on the other— these are the two poles between which human creative instinct swings in an everlasting rhythm. And as human life attains new forms over and over again in the everlasting tension between Liberty and Law, so in the realm of art, the polarity of creative impulse causes perennial changes in structure and a constant transformation of forms. Being well aware of this polarity, we use, to characterize it, a varying terminology: realism and idealism, naturalism and stylism, the particular and the universal. And we distinguish times, nations, even whole epochs of civilization by whichever of these two tendencies of creative instinct is predominant.

The highest creations of art, however, the great masterpieces, distinguished and honored by the name of classic, arise in those rare moments of history, when in a people or in a man these two opposing tendencies of creative instinct come to a harmonious adjustment; where sense and thought, emotion and reason counterbalance each other. Said Friedrich Schiller in one of his essays on esthetics: "It is only when in the midst of all the changes of which the imagination is susceptible, reason maintains its rule— it is only then that the divine or the ideal is manifested." In literature, for instance, such great moments appeared with Dante, with Shakespeare and Goethe; in painting with Giotto; in music with Johann Sebastian Bach. These great artists succeeded in merging the two divergent forces of mind to a harmonious whole, thus, as exceptional individuals, demonstrating a complete integration of liberty and law. In architecture, a similar integration has been realized only once in the course of its history: in the Doric temple, wherein the harmonious spirit of the Greek has created a form that for its perfection became, in fact, the esthetic pattern, the classic model and measure, for all time to come.

DUALISM OF FORMS

From this immanent dualism of man's creative instinct, there was derived that dualism of forms which is to be found throughout the history of Western art. If we distinguish classicism, meaning ancient art and its later revival, the art of the Renaissance, from Gothic and Baroque, we really distinguish with those terms two different species of forms. Raphael and Mathias Grünewald, though they are contemporaries, are guided by different concepts of form. When both painted the same theme, the transfiguration of Christ, Raphael, in his famous picture in the Vatican, gave a strong composition of figures, arranged in well-balanced symmetry, and the masses in complete equilibrium. Grünewald's picture, however, which formed a wing of the great altar at Isenheim, is a tempest of emotion, a movement of floating and soaring lines, expressing the exaltation and mystery of the biblical miracle.

The contrast between these two pictures representing the same scene is a consequence not so much on the difference of national characters, but mainly of the different attitudes to the problem of form. What is meant by that is to be seen even more clearly if we compare two buildings, such as a palace of the Renaissance, let us say, the Palazzo Strozzi in Florence, with a medieval castle, the Castle of Nuremberg, for example. In its irregular form, the Castle of Nuremberg, a huge mass of buildings, does not seem to be planned at all, but to have grown wild, built up by the dynamics of nature that continue to act in its structure. The outlines of the building, erected on a steep

8

hill, adapt themselves to the natural conditions of the site: they cling to all the ledges of the rugged rock; and like a plant that draws its nourishment out of its environment, out of the accidents and conditions of its existence, this building seems in the act of adjusting itself to its life-space. The purpose of the building is to serve as a shelter and defense. And its structure is developed out of the functions it has to serve. In its forms, each part of this building is determined and adapted to the particular demands it has to fulfill. It is due to this underlying concept that the building shows an irregular structure. Its form is dynamic like all forms of organic growth, and full of individual character like all creations of nature.

Now, when we look at the Renaissance palace, its form, in contrast to the medieval castle, shows complete regularity. Its plan presents a figure of regular outline, its rooms are grouped around a rectangular system of axes, its structure forms a simple cube and its façades are founded on a symmetrical design, accenting the middle part by the dominating architecture of the main entrance door. The walls are divided into regular sections by grouping the windows at equal intervals. The purpose of the building is also to serve as a shelter and defense. However, in bringing this demand into form, the individual necessities were subordinated to a general law, to the geometric law of regularity and symmetry. Even in setting and placing the building, every accidental character of the site had to yield to the rigid rules of the geometric law. It is from such a concept that the building obtained its static form, representing a general type derived from an abstract principle of order.

The same dualism of forms is revealed in the art of town planning. There is the irregular town "with streets curled as fancy dictated, wandering along the foot or the scarp of a range of hills, following the ridge of winding downs, and only by chance stumbling briefly into straightness." But this seemingly fanciful irregularity is not the result of a haphazard growth, affording by chance the gratification of picturesque effects, but the product of the most deliberate building, adapting each part of the town to the topographical conditions of the site. On the other hand, there is the regular town, the plan of which is based on a pre-determined system without regard for the topography of the site and the natural contingencies.

The city of Edinburgh offers a spectacular example in which both the regular and the irregular form are to be found side by side. The city is located on a group of hills between which lies a ravine that once contained a lake. The oldest part of the city sprang up round Edwin's castle, built on one of the rocky hills in the south. From this castle a main thoroughfare, the High Street, descends to the foot of the valley, and around it developed the medieval town, its narrow streets and alleys following the contours of the site and presenting a most picturesque sight with their irregular lines and winding curves. When in the eighteenth century the town began to extend over the northern hills beyond the intersecting valley, the new parts, in accordance with the ideas of classicism, were laid out on a regular plan. A network of straight streets crossing at right angles and interrupted by large plazas of geometrical form, was imposed on the hilly site, affording to the new town an architectural regularity, sharply contrasting with the picturesque irregularity of the medieval parts. But the regularity, obtained at the price of a conflict with the topographical conditions, in this case had somewhat dubious results: the streets in the new town climb up the hills in steep grades, and the regular squares and circles, developed along the slopes, looking like plates on an inclined tray, give the impression that they will glide off the next moment.

These examples illustrate that the development of Western art, as is stated in Goethe's distinction between formative and fine art, is marked by a dualism of forms. Its history moves between these two poles of the regular and irregular, of the static and the dynamic form. Both forms exist side by side, often even at the same time, independent of the changing modes of ornament and decoration which indicate the succession of styles. It is not that one develops out of the other: each of these types has its own evolution, producing buildings of high perfection, each after its kind. And the history of art is the history of these masterpieces.

ORGANIC AND MECHANICAL ORDER

Whether regular or irregular, static or dynamic, all form is a final result of the desire for order. To build is to make a plan. To plan is to follow a definite concept of order.

In accordance with the dualism of the creative instinct and the antithesis of intuitive and constructive imagination, we find followed in building two different principles of order: one that takes the structure as an organism; growing on its own according to the proper and immutable law of its individual existence;

11

adapted to its function and environment, as a plant or any other living organism grows, developing itself in its proper life-space. Then, in contrast to this principle, we find another idea of order taking the structure as mechanism, composed of various elements put into order according to the immutable law of a system *a priori*. Viewing these two different concepts of the problem of structure, we speak of organic order as opposed to mechanical order.

In building, the immutable law followed by mechanical order is based on Geometry. As a practical art, Geometry was founded by the Egyptians. Promoted later by the Greeks to a system of thinking, it is one of the oldest sciences invented by the human mind, and is used to understand and explain the universe as a system of order. Space and number, as ideas of the unchangeable and immutable, were early abstracted from reality, and as fixed principles of the infinite and absolute set against the fluctuation of appearances and the variations of individual life.

Not before Geometry had been invented had that art come into being which is called *Architecture*. It is probably safe to say that the first creation which deserves this name was the Pyramid. The divine will that the Egyptians saw, or read into the Universe, was manifested in their mathematical concept of the world's order. And this concept was represented in their social order, symbolized in the static form of the pyramid. The broad basis supporting the structure of this feudal society is formed by the great masses of the working people. The pyramidal building of society, then, grades up in a large hierarchy of classes to the small caste of the priesthood, and finally culminates in the point at the summit, which symbolizes the king-priest reaching into the sky. This is architecture in its primal state, developed into a true symbol. All architecture is based on Geometry, limited to the ideas of space and number, and in the course of its development it has become more and more devoted to the glorification of mathematical laws, based on a system of lasting measures and demonstrating its canon of proportions.

But older than Architecture is *Building*. The rise of architecture as a fine art already presupposes a high degree of civilization. The impulse to build, however, is inborn in man, rooted in his fundamental impulses toward protection and nurture. Building, as creative art, belongs to the beginning stages of civilization. The primitive man builds, as the peasant and the farmer still do in present times: they do not know about architecture. Their structures, their houses and barns, are built according to the daily needs of life, the limitations set by available materials; and they are joined to soil and nature. Language shows its sensitiveness in distinguishing this primary creative activity of man by the good popular folkword *to build,* from that later artistic production for which it uses the learned word *Architecture.* "Throughout the history of civilization," said Patrick Geddes, "it is the peasant who is *par excellence* the builder—as the Germanic word *Bauer* in its double meaning of builder and peasant, aptly recalls." All indigenous building is organic in structure: it develops its forms after the fashion of organic nature, which produces new forms over and over again, developing each of its creations into its own individual character. To build is to create organisms the form of which, in their particular individuality, is determined by the principles involved in the law of their internal growth.

THE PROBLEM OF ORDER TODAY

With these principal differentiations in mind, let us now look at our own situation. Our time, there is no doubt, must be characterized as a period of crisis. The fundamental change of economic conditions taking place under the insignia of industrialization and mechanization, has shaken social order in its foundations. A complete transformation of life is taking place. Wherever we look, at the state or the people, at economics or society, at science or art, fundamental changes are in process. A world of obsolete forms and institutions is coming to an end, another slowly struggles into existence. With violent concussions, that everlasting spectacle of dying and growing is taking place again on the stage of the world. With combat and convulsion the old forms of order are broken to pieces. With intense resistance the emancipation from traditional habits of law is carried through; emancipation from forms that once were original and full of life, but which in the course of historical evolution have lost their primary meaning and their relationship to life. Reluctantly, but at last, the discussion is opened on the changed reality that forms our environment. And in the course of this great historical act, arousing our sympathy and provoking immediate participation, we realize the constructive forces of a new spirit that will stamp, like the stage director behind the scene, man, society and the form of a new civilization to come.

Forces of a new spirit! It is, indeed, a fundamental change in

thinking that is revealed in the reconstruction of life now performed by the human mind. Wherever the primary problem of
structure is thought of anew, it is thought of in concepts related
to organic life, to man and nature. "Science," said the English
philosopher A. N. Whitehead, "is taking on a new aspect in
our time. It is becoming a study of organisms." Guided by this
idea of organism, the human spirit, ever active and advancing,
begins to think of new forms which are once again suitable for
our organic existence. The disastrous conditions into which an
excessive rationalism and a humiliating mechanism have forced
our natural existence have awakened a new longing for nature,
have called forth a desire to be nearer to the sources of life. A
complete reversal of the outlook on life is taking place in these
times: we see another approach of man to nature, this time however, not in the sentimental spirit of a Rousseau, but in accordance with the strict teachings of science and technique which
have revealed the idea of organism, and have opened to us, in
this way, the wonder of creation and life anew.

Wherever the manifold forms of human institutions are
thought of anew, there they are conceived in a biological sense,
they are thought of in terms of organic structure. Among these
institutions, society first needs a new order, a problem now
under passionate discussion. Its solution is still to be worked
out, and the structure that society will embrace in the future
can now hardly be foretold. But from the new mode of thinking based on the idea of organism, we may expect a transformation that leads from a static structure of society, built up in di-
verse classes, to a dynamic structure: to an organic order in

which the position of the individual, and therefore his social status as well, is determined by the function he serves for the whole. In political economy, the new ideas of structure are already advancing in the spheres of social and economic planning, where economic activity is no longer considered under the aspect of private profit only, but as a social function, as a service for the community. Finally, in politics there is also a change of ideas in process: a general discussion has gone on since the World War as to whether the traditional principle of static structure in the relationship between the nations, implied in the political term of the "Balance of Power," could be replaced by another principle of organic order called "The Society of Nations," thought of as an organization guaranteeing the welfare of the commonwealth by organic co-operation of all its members.

It is a new spirit, and also a new mood, another temper of the soul that is announced in these changed ideas of structure. Rooted in conscience, they proclaim a new direction of will, and based on the ethics of service, they establish new ideas of value. These new ideas may not yet be strong enough to perform a complete change of the social order; they are, however, constantly permeating reality: struggling against traditional forms and obsolete ideas, and gradually gaining credit and influence, they are transforming the world carried over from the past into that which will express our new potentialities.

It is this conflict of two opposing ideas of order that causes the bewildering crisis and the baffling social unrest we have to live through in these times. And in this crisis of order, in this change of structural thinking, there is also rooted the present

16

crisis in the art of building. It is before the problem of order that minds begin to diverge. At the present time, the two opposing ideas of order discussed in the previous paragraphs still exist side by side. Their particular nature and action is to be seen in the traditional forms of academic architecture, and the new structures, produced by the spirit of modern building. Drawing our conclusions from these initial creations, which announce the coming of a new style, we are entitled to believe that the creative human instinct, in the continuous rhythm of its movements, is swinging again to another pole.

PART ONE

THE RISE OF A NEW SPIRIT
IN BUILDING

1. FLOWERING AND FADING
OF THE CLASSICAL TRADITION

THE BEGINNING OF REVIVALISM

Architecture, as a fine art based on Geometry and limited to the ideas of number and space, celebrated its highest triumphs in the time of the Renaissance. Opening again the buried sources of classical culture, this period accomplished the revival of Graeco-Roman art. The Renaissance, seen from a sociological point of view, "produced the educated class, and within it the perfect individual, the State of absolute sovereignty, the *salon* and the academies"; it also inaugurated the rise of a new style in architecture, a style that found its fostering soil in the social conditions thus characterized, and growing from this soil rose to world-wide authority.

The architecture of the Renaissance, said Jakob Burckhardt, its famous historian, is a derivative style that voluntarily expressed its thoughts in a foreign language. It came to a climax, however, in a creation entirely of its own: in the central dome which is the highest realization of the idea of space. This idea of self-contained space, the beauty of which rests on its static form, its complete balance and the perfect harmony of its proportions, reached its culmination point with the building at Rome of St. Peter's Cathedral, crowned by Michelangelo's masterly dome. This monumental architecture, never surpassed in greatness, is an impressive symbol, representing to all Christendom the idea of *ecclesia triumphans*.

The style of the Italian Renaissance inaugurated a new age in architecture. In the further development of its ideas, however, during the seventeenth and eighteenth centuries, France took the final part. It was not by accident that it was precisely France, the classical country of order by reason, which achieved the culmination of classicism. The French adopted the great example with alacrity and enthusiasm, and absorbed the new ideas spreading from Italy with the readiness of a kindred race. Penetrating these ideas with that specific French spirit—that spirit of reason which dominates all branches of life in that country—they not only succeeded in modernizing the Italian pattern; but, subduing the style to method and principle, they also created the doctrine of classicism, conferring on the style that superior self-certainty which protected it from all temptations, particularly from the rising influence of Roman Baroque, with its new tendency to set space in flow and motion.

When in 1664, in preparing a design for the remaining east portion of the Louvre, a competition was held by Colbert, he invited, along with a group of French architects, some of the leading Baroque masters of Rome, such men as Rainaldi, Borromini, Pietro da Cortona and Lorenzo Bernini. The following year Bernini came to Paris, received with almost royal honors, and soon produced a new project, designed in the brisk and soaring forms of his impetuous style, breaking all academic rules and defying all acknowledged laws of measure and proportion. His

CLASSICAL PARIS

The great axis starting from the court of the Louvre, crossing the Place de la Concorde, running up the Avenue des Champs Elysées with the Arc de Triomphe as a terminal vista. (*Compagnie Aérienne Française*)

INTERIOR OF THE GREAT EXHIBITION, London, 1851

HARPERS BUILDING, New York

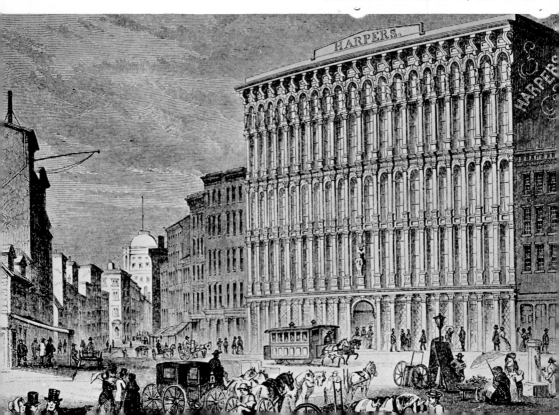

project was, of course, disapproved, and after his departure superseded by Perrault's grand colonnade of Corinthian order, breathing in its clearness, correctness and dignity the spirit of the classical tradition and in its absolute unity the tendencies of the time.

It is in France, not in Italy, that the new style of architecture, developed with the rise of the Renaissance, gained the utmost freedom in the use of its artistic means. Here it was that its diction became smoother and more fluent, more flexible and versatile; that its form grew more elegant and more cosmopolitan. The French, in fact, succeeded in transforming the classic style of architecture revived with the Renaissance, into a new style of display that acquired international validity. The French first of all developed classicism into a world-wide style of almost unlimited applicability. As French became the universal language of court and society at this time, so classicism became the universal taste in architecture generally followed all over the world.

THE APOTHEOSIS OF CLASSICISM: PARIS

In Paris the authority of classicism was founded, and it was Paris, which in its central part is one of the most brilliant creations of classicism, that set its superscription on the style and led it on its triumphal march through the world.

Modern Paris is developed on a plan the main lines of which were designed under the reign of *Le Roi Soleil* and his successors. In the centuries that saw the idea of absolute sovereignty rising and reaching its culmination, Paris, the center of this idea, was embellished with a great number of pompous avenues and monumental plazas. At this time were built the series of inner Boulevards, the Place des Victoires and the Place Vendôme, both designed by Jules Hardouin Mansart, and the Place de la Concorde, an incomparable piece of architectural *mise en scène,* designed by J. A. Gabriel, First Architect to the King: a kind of garden plaza forming the transition from the regular gardens of the Tuileries to the open landscape of the Champs Elysées.

On one end, towards the River Seine the large square is closed by the Palais Bourbon, on the other end by two stately buildings with identical façades, the Twin Palaces, designed by Gabriel, framing the entrance to the Rue Royale and focusing the view to the Madeleine Church which forms the terminal vista for the plaza. Each of these monumental plazas, following one another in a pompous parade, offers a perfect example demonstrating the architectural principles of classicism: its tendency towards geometric regularity and symmetry, towards norm and measure, its longing for the self-contained space resting in full repose, balanced in the perfect harmony of its proportions.

And in this plan of Paris, there is also developed that great main axis, running parallel to the Seine, that became the backbone of the modern city. Starting its course from the court of the Louvre, which forms the ideal center of the plan, and pushing forward with tremendous power, this great axis opens the view upon an architectural spectacle that, bringing the fascinating splendor of the city into focus, puts all the world under its alluring spell over and over again. The eye, strongly directed by this powerful guiding line, glides over the green parterre of the Tuileries gardens in the foreground, with their bubbling fountains and flowing waters; it then follows the straight course of the Avenue des Champs Elysées, starting beyond the Place de la Concorde and gently rising to its top, the Place de l'Etoile with the Arc de Triomphe in its center. In this monumental building the impulsive force of the main axis is once more concentrated, just a moment before dismissing its bursting energy, like an exploding skyrocket, into a bundle of minor streets radiating from this center. And as beyond the plaza the ground falls away, so from afar the view through the wide opening of the Arc de Triomphe leads into the indefinite expanse of the horizon.

Modern Paris, indeed, presents the apotheosis of classicism, exhibiting the potentialities of architecture as a fine art. This Paris of Classicism is an architectural spectacle arranged in masterful fashion—a pompous show consisting of a continuous series of monumental plazas and broad avenues, gracefully interrupted by entertaining *entr'actes* in form of spacious parks and public gardens. Within the splendid framework of this enchanting scene, there appear, like actors on the stage, many magnificent buildings, isolated or arranged in a well-composed group, but always intimately connected with, and related to, one another by a co-ordinating system of geometrical axes. These monumental buildings appear in richly adorned vestments, they use a solemn and dignified language, and talk in a moving and declamatory tone; and with their ceremonial attitude they play their dumb part *"A toutes les gloires de France."*

Voltaire once said that it is the task of art to increase the fame of the King, the splendor of the Court, and the welfare of the

State. With Paris as setting, classicism has accomplished one of the most imposing exemplifications of that statement. As a style whose principles are based on an abstract law imposed upon reality, classicism reveals the complete identity of the concept of art with that of the state then in existence. In the state of absolutism even art is supposed to render homage to the sovereign power. In fact, the architecture of classicism is grand, even unsurpassable in all those qualities which at this time state and society demanded of art: qualities characterized in French as *grandeur—élégance—représentation.*

With the creation of eighteenth-century Paris, classicism was at the zenith of its destiny. Full of admiration, the world looked, from then on, at the French capital, enchanted as well as bewitched by its glamor and glare. With the pattern of Paris, it seems, a universal and popular taste was created to which the whole world was ready to surrender. Let it be added that this pattern, with its wide streets, broad avenues, and circular plazas, in many respects anticipated the needs of that new rationalistic mode of life which became characteristic of modern urbanism. As a matter of fact, in eighteenth-century Paris, certain needs of the modern metropolis were already satisfied long before, in the course of the Industrial Revolution, they were actually felt. Take all these facts together, and you have the reasons for the immense and never-ceasing influence spreading from Paris through the whole civilized world up to the present time.

THE CODIFICATION OF THE ACADEMIES

It is due to the example of Paris that the spirit of classicism has triumphed over and over again. For three centuries, the esthetic doctrine of the style, although frequently impeached and strongly opposed, kept its supreme authority in the domain of city planning, landscape architecture, and architecture.

This doctrine, however, was worked out by the academies. Founded as professional schools, these new institutes of science and learning carried on a new kind of scientific training in art, which, since the time of the Renaissance, has replaced the old honorable apprenticeship of trades and crafts as it was practiced in the Middle Ages. During the seventeenth and eighteenth centuries, the leading architects of France, Perrault and D'Aviler, Blondel and Briseaux, tried to establish a universal doctrine of architecture based on the incontestable laws of Geometry, on the fixed principles of number and measure. The midday of classicism is filled with continuous efforts to find out the secret of proportions and to raise it to the sphere of mathematical laws accessible to reason. The greatest endeavors were made to frame the principles of geometric order into a canon of final rules that can be taught as well as learned.

This doctrine, once established, was supposed to be infallible. It formed, from then on, the norm and measure of production as well as of criticism. It is in its name that judgment is passed in all matters of taste. All artistic production is subdued to its rules and regulations. Every problem of building is now thought of in terms of the doctrine; all planning is based upon a system

27

a priori abstracted from the laws of Geometry. To that system of co-ordinate axes, as the guiding principle of esthetic composition, was deliberately sacrificed, without any scruple, all regard for use, for immediate service to life. Even the organic growth of nature was entirely subjected to the authority of abstract law. It is with the doctrine of classicism that the French style of landscape architecture came into origin: in the regular garden (that new pattern created by André LeNôtre), with its trelliswork, cut lawns and groves formed of trimmed hedges, the rigidity of the doctrine is shown in its last consequences.

THE DECAY OF THE CLASSICAL TRADITION

After the society that had initiated the rise of classicism had been toppled over in the tempest of the French Revolution, it was the academies that kept alive, not so much the esthetic values of the style, but its theory. Handed down by these schools from generation to generation, the doctrine of classicism lives on into our times. But cut off from the soil in which it was once embedded, detached from the social conditions from which it received its driving power, the tradition of classicism became an empty husk, a surviving adornment of a social state long passed away. As a merely academic doctrine, the classical tradition from the Napoleonic period on led an isolated life, a life, so to speak, *in vacuo*. The spirit was definitely gone. The classical tradition itself began to fade.

The architectural forms accepted in ready-made shape were no longer understood in their functional meaning, but used as handy elements in the artificial game of composition. With

28

the rise of the academic theory, however, the ground-plan began to lead an artistic life of its own: the plan, from then on, was considered and designed to be a geometric ornament. In the present time this sort of planning, as an art in itself, is still cultivated at the Ecole des Beaux Arts at Paris. "The plan," said Le Corbusier, criticizing the esthetic formalism of that mode of planning, "has become a piece of paper on which black marks for walls and lines for axes play at a sort of mosaic on a decorative panel making graphic representations of star-patterns, creating an optical illusion. The most beautiful star becomes the Grand Prix de Rome."

This esthetic game of geometric composition is continued in designing the façades: the surface is divided into regular sections by a number of axes following each other at equal intervals, and it is then decorated with architectural details of style-forms accepted in ready-made shape. These standard forms applied in a merely decorative, not in a functional sense, constitute the only substantial element of that esthetic game, and it is just this element which in the further development proves to be variable and most susceptible to change. After classicism had once made autonomous the forms and ornamentation taken over from ancient architecture, and utilized these historical forms to represent new contents of life, the whole treasure of inherited forms was gradually set free; and this inheritance was heartily welcomed by the academic school as a means of enriching their compositions. Once the Renaissance had pointed the way to the revival of an historical style, the nineteenth century, then, took the next step on this path by the Gothic revival in architecture, accomplished in the era of Romanticism. This era, with its broad extension of man's mental horizon, produced a general "historicizing" of thought and evolved a fresh sensitivity to all past cultures, even to the most foreign of them. This evolution, in its consequences, led in architecture to the concept of the historical styles as independent entities. With the Gothic revival, the other basic form element of Western architecture was made independent, leading from then on an existence, so to speak, *in abstracto*.

With the progressive breaking of social bonds in the further course of the nineteenth century, with the collapse of standards and traditional value-concepts under the economic and social transformation, there set in that unconfined individualizing of thought and feeling, characteristic of the modern age, from which arose the critical problems of its art and culture. While at the beginning of the century, in the period of Greek revival, academic architecture was still based on a common ideal of culture, providing an unquestionable accord at least on problems of art, this common ideal began to waver, finally making room for the boldest subjectivism. This attitude abolished every homogeneous standard of judgment, and introduced a fateful anarchy into all questions of taste. It is in this way that the architecture of the nineteenth century, after having tried one historical style after another, finally ended at an extensive eclecticism, which greedily and without any scruple devoured the architectural forms and ornaments produced the whole world over. And finally architectural production grew stiff in a barren formalism.

WILLIAM MORRIS: FLAT PATTERNS

"Dove and Rose"; "Squirrel"; and "Cherwell"

CITY HALL, STOCKHOLM, Ragnar Ostberg, architect
(Courtesy Swedish Travel Information Bureau)

TRIANGLE, Washington, D. C., 1933 *(Courtesy World Wide Photos)*

SHOPPING AMONG THE STYLES

This formalistic eclecticism is still in vogue, and favored by the popular taste. And there are many varieties of this modern species of academic architecture. In its production it follows some tradition of choice corresponding to personal tastes and convictions. These varieties range from a dry and formalistic style-architecture merely imitating the historical patterns, to those free and ingenious productions, in which the inherited forms are felt afresh, and, filled with the inventive spirit of the architect, sometimes regain their original character. It is from the virtuosoship of architectural design that these buildings gain their particular charm and their sensuous effect, which never fail to suit the ordinary taste. And the eclecticist is on intimate terms with his public; he is, so to speak, the artist of the *juste milieu,* keeping ready for each project a solution that will satisfy everybody's taste. For the house of the bourgeois he uses the Georgian or Colonial pattern, skilfully adapting it to modern needs; and for public buildings he follows the great examples of classicism, debasing the heroic character of that style into a cheap allegory of power and domination. Some vague idea of Napoleonic imperialism is impressed upon the naïve spectator who views the new buildings of the Government of the United States erected at Washington in 1934: a group of office buildings of modern steel construction, but blinded with classicistic façades forming an endless parade of columns (and with rooms behind these pompous façades so dark that at noon of a bright winter day the lights have to be turned on).

The eclecticist, then, never takes a risk: he always keeps the beaten but safe track of academic doctrine, carefully avoiding any kind of experiment. In the face of the audacious adventures to which the spirit of modern building always braces itself, the eclecticist pretends to be the reliable expert of the profession, the appointed guardian and Lord Keeper of its·traditional craftsmanship. In fact, the eclecticist is well acquainted with all the tricks and knacks of the profession, and his *routine d'atelier* is not easily to be surpassed. It is he who is at home with all the arts of esthetic detail: he has a good sense of color and decoration, and he knows how to design and use ornaments. In short, he is strong, even unassailable in all those things that can be taught and learned, and his professional skill consists merely of qualities which can be acquired by artistic training and by cultivation of taste, power of judgment and critical faculty. Where such qualities are deemed sufficient, his accomplishments are beyond competition. Owing to the high standard of his esthetic culture, he achieves in his production a sensuous effect frequently lacking in modern buildings, which as yet scarcely go beyond the merely utilitarian form.

By their quantity the works of modern eclecticism still determine the architectural aspect of our cities. Perhaps the most exemplary, certainly the most brilliant, work of this school is the new City Hall in Stockholm, designed by Ragnar Ostberg: a building in which the motives of the national building tradition and the forms of sundry historical styles are composed into an effective whole delightful to the eye. Its picturesque effect is enhanced by its location on the wide water plane of Lake Malaren, a location which recalls that of the Ducal Palace at Venice, of whose architecture the new City Hall at Stockholm, opening with wide arcades on the water front, is manifestly suggestive.

ECLECTICISM: AN ART FOR ART'S SAKE

It is, however, the weakness of this eclecticism, as of all kinds of academic art, that it is affected by no other than esthetic problems. Their representatives come to art only by way of art; and their love for art is antipathetic to the ingenuous experience of reality. At the most, they would look at this reality from an esthetic point of view, too. Now, as it is only the decay of their academic concept of art that they are able to discover in that reality, they try to escape this crude reality by reaching back to the historical form. It offers itself as a finished shape in an unfinished and shapeless present; it opens up in such apparently practical ways a prospect of getting past the crisis that everywhere exists in the realm of order and form. Taken out of the past and, thereby, out of the circumstances which conditioned its origin and content, it still offers the architect a useful artistic means, a means, moreover, of tested effectiveness and of almost universal applicability. There clings to the historic form, by reason of the atmosphere peculiar to it, an intangible element giving access to "those higher influences of historic, artistic and poetic purposes," which Karl Friedrich Schinkel was convinced must not be lacking, in order to elevate the work to the level of art. By continuous freshening and skilful mingling of these varied effective factors, it is often possible to conceal the graceless reality and, by aid of historical tradition, to get up a sort

33

of make-believe culture, covering the nakedness of a reality deemed inimical to art.

The eclecticist, in fact, makes a virtue of overlooking reality and the practical needs of modern life, anaesthetizing his intelligence with the artistic finish of his form. By this one-sided cult of art, however, form—exalted into an end in itself—finally began to lead a life of its own, detached from its original conception and content. In the present, however, it is just the content that is undergoing a fundamental change: under the pressure of the new problems, rising up from all sides out of the changed social and economic conditions, the whole content of life is in a state of ferment. With these fundamental changes, however, the former integration of form and content is broken up.

Now, the more extreme the tension becomes between the values of form and the demands of use, the more the form itself is doomed to decay. When in a design an historical style is correctly followed and its purity and integrity is faithfully preserved, the conformity to its original concept is frequently attained at the cost of use. When the design of your house is based on the principles of geometric order and, for the effect of the façade, the windows are arranged at equal intervals, according to the system of axes, you will often find your rooms badly lighted and unsatisfactorily accommodated to exposure, and in cases so frequently noticed, where, from respect for the prerogatives of the axis, the window is placed right in the corner, close to the partition wall, you will have difficulty in finding a satisfying arrangement for your furniture. When, however, complying with modern demands, which involve a change of structure,

the architect of the historical school gives way to use and purpose, he must inevitably strike against the principles of his
chosen traditional form. As a matter of fact, the sensuous beauty
of academic architecture, in its eclectic varieties, is in danger
of being blasted from within by the change of structure that is
going on under the pressure of modern needs.

Eclecticism is characteristic of an ending period. Eclectic architecture may still be able to produce variations but it affords
no prospect of further evolution. This sort of art is a typical
product of decay: no longer able to produce new forms of its
own, it uses up for its esthetic purposes the remnants of bygone
cultures. It is characteristic that it is in just the United States, at
present, that this sort of academic eclecticism celebrates its highest triumphs. Vestiges of the Colonial spirit, lurking still in the
national taste, find naïve satisfaction in an architecture adorned
with the treasures of old-world forms. It is not by accident that
among the students of the Beaux Arts the numerical superiority
is American. It is the excellent training in design and decorative
detail bestowed by this institute that provides the superior qualities of polish and refinement distinguishing the works of the
academic school in this country.

The attitude of the academic school is a purely esthetic one.
It is admitted that for certain talents this attitude is the only
one making possible the realization and development of their
specific faculties. Afraid of a merciless reality not yet offering
the foothold of a tradition, these talents seek support in a selected historical tradition. The motives behind this attitude are
revealed with ruthless frankness in the statements of that letter-

writer in the concluding chapter of Dostoevsky's novel *Raw Youth*. In view of the lack in his day of settled types, he declared that, were he a writer of romances, he would certainly choose his heroes from the tradition of the old nobility. For only in the culture of this social rank would it still be possible "to find at least that outward semblance of fine order and esthetic beauty so necessary in a novel to produce an artistic effect on the reader." In these types, he continues, there would actually be found everything that has been brought to some sort of perfection anyway. He expressly adds that he does not say this because he is accepting unconditionally the truth and justice of that beauty. That is a secondary question. What to his mind seems of most consequence is the finality of the forms and the existence of some sort of order. And what matters most of all for us, he says, is to have any sort of order.

In the disordered times the modern architect and his patron have to live in, they find refuge on a remote island, where they can live under the law of authoritative forms and under the protection of an order no longer to be found elsewhere. On the other hand, it is not to be denied that the works of modern eclecticism, as purely esthetic conceptions, fall decidedly short of meeting the requirements of a changing age. They are produced in the ivory-tower, where the cries of social needs and the demands of their problems are never heard of. Modern eclecticism is, par excellence, an art for art's sake, an attitude of mind which, during the nineteenth century, led painting and sculpture to a new flowering. With the same attitude, however, architecture, which must think of its form rather from the standpoint of the community than from the individual, became detached from the native soil from which alone it can draw nourishment for its growth. Fading, therefore, it was replaced, in the nineteenth century, by an academic substitute of merely imitative character.

2. STATING THE PROBLEM

The nineteenth century at its beginning was burdened with the glorious inheritance of the classical tradition. But with this century, called the century of technical progress, there soon arose new problems and practical needs, which were no longer to be mastered after the fashion imposed by the classical doctrine. There came an early awakening to the fact that machine technique, bringing something wholly new into the world, was destined to overthrow the traditional forms of life and society. It was also soon perceived that an architecture using the historical styles, as if to express living thoughts in a dead language, was unworthy of the creative spirit of the new epoch. Impulsive artists came to rebel against the fate of being epigones. Brought up in the doctrine of classicism, they soon perceived that the mere exploitation of the inherited treasure of historical forms in itself could not generate new ideas. Venerable ideals, inherited as part of a great tradition achieved in the past, when repeated under conditions so entirely changed, could only be debased into mere conventions—even when these ideals were recalled with the most noble and faithful of intentions.

The rise of a new spirit in building goes back to the early decades of the nineteenth century. In 1824, Karl Friedrich

Schinkel designed the Berlin Museum, whose Greek columnar façades gave a monumental expression to the classic epoch of Goethe. But at this very time, when the Greek Revival was in full bloom, the same architect wrote the following: "It would be a sorry thing for architecture, and it would not deserve its rank in the circle of the other arts, if all the individual parts developed in ancient times—such as the orders of columns and the kinds of moldings—were filed away, and nothing were left to imagination but to make some new combination of these ready-made forms. A scanty matter for reason!"

A few years later, the same architect went to England on a study-journey. Passing through the new industrial districts, he frequently encountered the brutal manifestations of the early age of steam-power. He went to Manchester and there saw the new factories, where people worked from fourteen to sixteen hours a day. The enormous masses of red brick, designed by mere foremen—showing no architecture, as he said, and erected only for the barest necessity—gave him a tremendous shock. Under the almost terrifying impression he received from these grimy monsters, of which he made a sketch in his note-book, he began to think of the fundamental changes that the new Industrial Age would produce in the whole social and mental life of man. And thinking particularly of the influence the new age would exert upon architecture, he wrote in his diary: "All great ages have left a record of themselves in their style of building. Why should we not try to find a style for ourselves?"—our own independent form, as he explains, which must start with a consideration of the life by which we are surrounded; a style that will find its greatest merit in adapting itself to a host of new inventions which have not as yet been utilized in an artistic manner.

With these prophetic words, Schinkel stated the architectural problem of his century. And as an architect, he also dealt with it practically. He undertook some important experiments, quite isolated in their time for their daring gallantry. Among these projects the audacious design for a proposed department-store to be erected in Berlin Unter den Linden, is perhaps the most advanced example. In its general form, the project did not wholly break away from historical convention, for Schinkel tried a synthesis of Gothic and Classic, of Northern and Antique form elements. But the spirit in which the problem was conceived and treated was quite new, and signified a beginning. The newness of conception appears in the bold design of the walls, providing large window openings, great areas of light-flooding glass. The principle on which this design is based is defined by the architect himself as follows: "Emphasize construction; use materials frankly; no useless parts; all clear and natural." That was, indeed, the language of a new century, the first manifestation of a new spirit in building.

Once the problem of a new style had been posed by Schinkel, the drive for its solution gave man no rest. There soon developed an inner spiritual movement that guided its discussion and passed it on from generation to generation up to the present day.

THE CHANGING STRUCTURE

Referring in his statement to the "new technical inventions" to be utilized in building, Schinkel showed that he understood the problem of a new style as one of structure—as primarily a morphological rather than an esthetic problem. In fact, these new inventions offered by modern technique caused a definite change from within, and it is with the use of new materials, such as iron and glass, that there first became visible a striking change of structure.

The use of iron for the purpose of construction offered two-fold advantage: less space was taken up than by the traditional stone work, and more light was admitted into the building. Used jointly with glass, the iron construction proved to be particularly fit to cover the large and wide-spanned halls now needed, such as track sheds for the new railroads, and market and exhibition halls coming into use with the rise of the modern city.

Iron construction was first used on a large scale when Henry Labrouste, architect-engineer, built the Bibliothèque Ste. Geneviève in Paris, in the middle forties. As a true representative of that new spirit which thinks first of the organism of each structure, the architect set up within the large reading-room of the Library an iron skeleton. The vertical posts are formed by slim columns of cast-iron, from which thin arched girders arise, gracefully perforated and adorned with delicate ornament. These serve as transverse arches for the two large barrel-vaults which cover the reading room. This form provides ample light and an uninterrupted expanse, both best serving the function of the room. The exterior of the building does not suggest the nature of the construction so frankly revealed in the interior. Here it seems as though the architect were still afraid of accepting the consequences involved in his courageous design. Sticking to his academic doctrine, he gave the building a rather dry façade with applied pilasters in the style of classicism. In this respect, Schinkel had already deviated much farther from the conventional pattern in his bold design for the proposed department store in Berlin. In his demonstrative project, the first instance of experimenting with wide wall openings and large areas of glass, the change of structure is more conspicuous; if executed, this building would have become a great sensation for his contemporaries.

Further experience in the new iron construction, then, was gained with the early works of engineering. Among them, the Halles Centrales in Paris, built in 1853 by Victor Baltard, was one of the advanced examples that gave a great impetus to modern building. In its full effect, however, the change of structure was first revealed to the astounded world with the Crystal Palace, erected in 1851 by Joseph Paxton for the Great International Exposition in London. It is worth noticing that the builder was not a professional architect, but a gardener who used his experience in designing greenhouses to build the great exhibition hall. In many cases throughout history it has been just the outsider, who, favored by his freedom from prejudices, has pushed forward the course of events. Using an iron skeleton closed with glass, Paxton erected a vast hall of airy lightness, the first dramatic instance of a reduction of the walls: changing their traditional function of a solid enclosing and weight-bearing mass into a thin transparent shell, bearing no weight, and indeed supported by the iron frame. With that structure the traditional idea of enclosed space, the dominant idea of classical architecture, is abandoned. It is supplanted by the idea of unlimited space: the world outdoors implied by the space within, a grand achievement that the new spirit of modern building would develop later on into a new architectural form expressing a new feeling toward life.

There was still another factor tending to transform the structure from within: that is the needs that made themselves felt with the development of modern comforts. Their growing pressure is to be noticed in the changed conception of planning. Schinkel erected for Wilhelm von Humboldt a new house in Tegel near Berlin, its design still based on the principles of the classical doctrine: the plan, developed in complete symmetry, is formed around a central axis, along which is also arranged a large open entrance hall. The first break with the classic ideal, as yet of exclusive authority and carefully guarded, was made by Ludwig Persius, a disciple of Schinkel, and the most gifted of his successors. He rejected the excessive passion for symmetry, which keeps the bulk of the building unbroken. This he did not for esthetic reasons, but because that passion, he said, restricted freedom in developing a useful and comfortable interior. With this argument he pushed on to the very heart of the problem, which goes far beyond a merely esthetic discussion and refers first, and in an elementary sense, to the problem of structure.

Persius built a great many houses in Potsdam and its environs, and in all his projects he emphasizes the individuality of each particular case, doing justice to the nature of each building and its special demands. He starts from the use each room has to serve, and he steadfastly tries to adapt the form and height of the room to its special function. He keeps to the principle of free grouping, in order to arrange the rooms according to their inner relationship. His plans are designed to provide the most favorable exposure to the sun, and to open to the rooms both the near prospect of the garden and the distant view of the surrounding landscape. As for the exterior, this kind of planning results in a structure the various parts of which, according to their purpose, are differentiated in their architectural appearance, in the height as well as in the form of their roofs. In the façades the different nature of the rooms is shown in the varied size and grouping of the windows, and in the form and arrangement of the necessary appurtenances, such as loggias, bay-windows and balconies. The buildings, clinging to the topographical contour of the site, are developed in intimate contact with their soil.

It is this regard for life and nature that gives the houses designed by Persius their simple charm and loveliness. In these well-formed houses, with their serene grace, there are already anticipated some of the ideas which much later, grown to full maturity, were realized in the work of Frank Lloyd Wright. In the architectural form Persius still adhered to historical patterns, but, aiming in his buildings at a more indigenous and popular effect, he preferred to go back to pre-classical styles: his forms and details are selected from Italian patterns of the romanesque period and from motives of the early Renaissance. As a rule, he used native materials found in the neighborhood where the building was to be erected. And he utilized these materials without concealment in a form of construction demanded by their nature.

The work of this new school of architecture, rising under the influence of Romanticism, has been appropriately termed *Landschafts-Architektur;* and for good reasons Persius, the founder of this school, was called the master of the architectural idyll. But one does no justice to the significance of Persius' work for the history of modern building if one limits oneself to a merely esthetic valuation, appreciating only the delightful effects of his ingenious eclecticism. It has often been noticed that in the art of Romanticism, which involves a great many heterogeneous elements, there is also implied a strong element of realism. This double tension of the era is clearly revealed in painting, and perhaps it can be best realized in the work of the French painter Géricault, certainly one of the most genuine representatives of the romantic temperament, whose paintings were infused with a strong naturalism. Persius, the architect, was a contemporary of a group of German painters that included such names as Otto Runge, Caspar David Friedrich, Carl Blechen and George Friedrich Kersting. The works of this group, who in their choice of subject prove true and typical exemplars of the romantic spirit, manifest an attitude of strict realism; and their realistic execution of subjects romantic in spirit has been characterized by one critic as *Stimmungs-Realismus,* which may be approximated in

45

translation by "realism with overtones." As for Persius, there is no doubt that he was in accord with the attitude of this new school of painting; he consciously joined the drift toward realism, manifesting a fundamental change in the mode of perception and thought, and giving rise, in logical consequence, to that basic change of structure which is to be noticed in building. It is in this sense that his work was felt and estimated as new by his contemporaries, notably in a study, published in Forster's *Allgemeine Bauzeitung,* on occasion of a memorial exhibition after his untimely death in 1845. This voluminous and not uncritical essay is, of course, rooted in the esthetic ideas of the time. The author characterizes the principle on which the work of Persius is based as "picturesque" in contrast to the "architectural" one of classicism. As in the meantime we have learned to make structure the starting point of all discussions on architecture, we must talk of "organic building" as opposed to the mechanic order of classicism based on an external Geometry. Though the essay still sticks to an old-fashioned terminology, the nature of the new principle is fully comprehended and clearly characterized with respect to its structural tendencies. Summing up the results of this new conception, the author said: "Arranging the parts of his buildings, Persius always followed the demand of use, and almost always the form truly corresponds to the particular nature of these parts: the halls show themselves as halls, the living rooms as real living rooms, both in their contrast and in their absolute form. The different sections of the building are so characterized that from the nature of the species is developed the entity of the individual room, a concept that

46

brings about the more differentiated contrast between hall and dining room, between living room and bed-room, between kitchen and servant room."

It is almost as if this contemporary criticism were groping for that new term "functionalism" which was to become the distinctive note of modern building.

SOCIAL IMPLICATIONS

While the structure was changing from within, the buildings were still dressed in a stylish drapery woven of historical forms and ornaments. The slender columns of cast-iron carrying the barrel-vault of the reading room in the Bibliothèque Ste. Geneviève, show a fine channeling, and end in Corinthian capitals, skilfully designed with a sharp pencil. When in the sixties the use of cast iron fronts, first employed by James Bogardus, became common in New York, the façades manifested a progressive change of structure: with the windows separated now only by narrow columns the walls began to shrink and the apertures to widen and to admit a larger amount of light. But the garniture of the iron columns still remained classic, its particular style to be freely chosen from the catalogue of the mill, according to personal taste. Architects had still to find the definite answer to Schinkel's question: "Why not a new style?"

To open the discussion of this problem anew, Maximilian, King of Bavaria, a friend of Schinkel and a sovereign interested in architecture, undertook a daring experiment. About the middle of the nineteenth century, he established a competition the object of which was precisely the invention of a new style. The

47

King believed that the time had finally come to utilize the products grown from the many seeds which thought had planted in the soil of art. "We are no longer living," reads the announcement of the competition, "in an era of intuitive creation from which in former times originated architectural order, but in an era of thought, research and self-conscious reflection. Architecture, however, proves to be wavering between classic and romantic ideas, both of them scarcely realized quite purely. The new forms produced with these ideas are transformations of the old ones. It is, however, a need of the human mind to strive for the new, and not only to imitate, with more or less perfection, the creations of the past. The basic idea of our epoch may be described as the striving for freedom, for free development and easy practice of physical and moral strength. Modern circumstances have changed the life of state and people. Should it not be possible to create a new style, to be developed, as once the Renaissance style was, out of traditional forms into new independent ones? Should it not be possible to create a new architecture adjusted in its forms to use and purpose; an architecture made of the old styles which the zeal of science has reconquered, but offering in its products a fine, harmonious and particular unity."

The announcement characterizes the mentality of the time and proves that even the problem of a new style could not be conceived in other than historical terms. The result of this well-meant attempt, of course, was a complete failure. For a style cannot be invented, it must grow naturally from the soil of an integrated society, as an expression of a new collective conscious-

48

ness. Thus, in the history of the spirit of modern building, there is to be found a long list of courageous pioneers, at the head of which is Karl Friedrich Schinkel, who not only came to an early understanding of the new problem, but also had a rather clear notion of the principles to be used in its solution. The record, indeed, is full of precocious experiments and daring advances into an unknown land, as it is also full of depressing failures and heroic defeats. To account for these, it has to be remembered that while the courageous pioneers saw and understood the new building problems, the time was not ripe for a solution to be attained. It is one thing to recognize a new problem; it is another to solve it, the possibility of a solution depending upon the time itself and its sociological conditions. An artistic idea, in the language of the sociologists, is only to be realized, when the social milieu is ready to accept it. Only when an idea is socially possible does it become a reality.

3. A MORAL REVOLUTION

If there is one thing that the history of modern building teaches, it is that all efforts to renew the art of building remain futile, until its roots begin to be firmly embedded in the freshly plowed soil prepared by the new social and economic forces. Look, for example, at the tragic fate of the Arts-and-Crafts movement started in England by John Ruskin and William Morris in the sixties. This reform movement was a moral crusade for an ideal of quality, as it sprang from their passionate indignation at a reckless and unruly industrialism, which not only disfigured the face of their beloved land, but which debased even the simplest objects of daily use. Interpreting the general decay of good taste as attendant on the rise of machine production, they turned their valiant front against the new economic forces, and mistaking the historical situation, attempted a restoration which aimed, in the name of quality, at a revival of craftsmanship and a return to craft handiwork.

We smile at their hopeless program for machine sabotage as a romantic enterprise of kindly intentions, framed in a fanatical esthetic concept. But the romantic enthusiasm with which the leaders of the movement conjured up the spirit of craftsmanship, sprang from a vital desire to enhance the quality of life rather than from a reactionary sentiment, as did for the greater part the morbid ideals of the Pre-Raphaelites who dominated English painting at that time. The Pre-Raphaelites' flight from the ugliness of modern life into an artificially harmonized world of images composed of such heterogeneous elements as medieval mysticism and protestant pietism was purely an esthetic reaction. But if Ruskin, with all the force of his glittering eloquence, praised Gothic art for its truth, honesty and naturalness; and if Morris, with his profound knowledge of the crafts of the Middle Ages, tried to re-enoble craftsmanship by a revival of its old techniques, the burning enthusiasm for their models was spent less on the esthetics of style and form than on the ethical and spiritual sustenance they believed them to contain.

Morris took it for granted that the breakdown of art in modern times was caused by the undermining of work-morale, and the decline of craft quality. Looking back at the Middle Ages, when handicraft was in full bloom, he found a code of labor that made the craftsman responsible for his product to the community, a responsibility obliging him to work on a principle of quality. The medieval guilds guaranteed this lofty work-morale by restricting the amount of work, on the basis that no workman should sacrifice craftsmanship to quantity or do more work than was needed to provide a living suitable to his social rank. In the medieval tradition of handicraft, Morris also found a concept of labor that gave man the pleasure of work by making it an expression of the whole individuality. Art, deeply embedded in handicraft, was the highest expression of man's pleasure in life and labor; it was "not luxury, it was right labor."

EARLY EVILS OF INDUSTRIALISM

This high ideal of work was shaken to its foundation by modern industrialism, which by its new processes broke the traditional unity between producer and product. The modern system of division of labor turned the workman into an operator of a machine, and as the machine does not turn out the whole of an article, but makes only a part of it, the workman is prevented from thinking of the product as a whole. Suppressing, by this mode of specialization, both the activity and expression of the whole individuality, the new system deprived the workman of the pleasure of labor, of the creative element in his work.

Now, under this new industrial system, what became of the product itself? In the age of handicraft the product grew simply, without any intermediary between the mind and the hand. Producer and product formed an integral unit in the system of work. Modern industrialism, breaking this integral unit by the principle of division of labor, placed between the workman and his product a new factor—the designer. However, it took a long time before the designer's task was really understood, and it was not before the end of the century that a new type of specialized industrial designer was educated. In the early days of Industrialism the designer was a man trained in ornamental design, and hired by the company to adorn the machine-made product with some cheerful and buoyant decorations copied from the sample-book of historical patterns. Having no understanding whatsoever of the process of production, the designer, given free hand, produced patterns suited neither to the material used for the product, nor to the tool used for its execution. Imitating the individual form of decoration which formerly flowed out of the manual work of the craftsman, he mistook the nature of the machine, which is strictly suited to standardized production only. In adding historical ornaments to the industrial article, he vulgarized the new goods, and also profaned the old ones, from which his patterns were copied. But it was believed that there is a common human desire for ornaments, and that it is too strong not to be satisfied. Thus, human ingenuity was misused to invent all sorts of machinery, tools and implements to produce stamped, punched, pressed ornaments. It is the substitute, shabby in form, and using cheap materials, that characterizes this early period of Industrialism.

The general debauchery of taste was first made public at the Great International Exposition in London, in 1851. The quality of the average products to be found on the market is to be judged from the Official Descriptive Catalogue. Here is a small selection of articles as described in the Catalogue:

"Imitations of flowers, made of paper, or modeled in wax, showing their applicability as ornaments for the drawing room."

"Specimens of stamped ornaments, used in the manufacture of lamps, chandeliers, etc., made from sheet or rolled metal."

"Specimens of painting, in imitation of various marbles, intended as substitute for marble in the construction of chimney-pieces, inlaying of tables etc."

"Imitations of various woods in painting."

"The *Day Dreamer,* an easy chair, decorated at the top with two winged thoughts—the one with bird-like pinions, and crowned with roses, representing happy and joyous dreams; the other with leathern bat-like wings—unpleasant and troublesome ones. Manufactured in papier-mâché, exhibited for its cheapness."

And so forth, other imitations and more substitutes, and at all events ornaments, fantastic and hideous, covering every square inch of the surface! In deploring the results of this destructive plague of ornament and imitation, Gottfried Semper, the German architect, after his visit to the London Exposition, wrote the following: "We have artists, but no art. England is the country of improvements: day by day new materials, new advances, new tools, new machines, new forces, are invented and adopted with enthusiasm. It is true, they accomplish a great deal, but at the cost of certain human faculties which will hardly be developed by the rationalistic mode as yet guiding the sciences, the leaders of the new present."

THE STORY OF THE RED HOUSE

This was the historical environment into which William Morris was born. He was twenty-five years old, and already well-known both in poetry and in art, when he first came face to face with the problem which decided his future career. The story of how he became a reformer of household art and decoration, is told at length in J. W. Mackail's *The Life of William Morris.* He had just been married and was about to build himself a house near London. Philip Webb made the design, and for its time, the planning was as original as was its material. It completely abandoned the type of the Italian stucco villa, the fashionable pattern of early Victorian, the type which Morris was fond of describing as a square box with a lid. "The name of Red House given to the new building was sufficient to describe it without ambiguity." Built in red brick and roofed with red tiles, it was the first attempt to re-establish the use of native building materials for the purpose of domestic building. The architect obviously did not care for purity of style in his design: he frankly used and mixed some reminiscences of Gothic and Baroque forms, such as the pointed arches and the high transom-windows of a small rectangular shape. He merely tried to give a homey and domestic character to the house, and to make it harmonious with its environment. "Externally the house was plain almost to severity; the decorative features it possessed were constructional, not of the nature of applied ornament." For its effect, it depended solely on the material, the color and the grouping of the masses; and the straight-forwardness in using and showing the material gave freshness and originality to the building.

In the history of modern building the Red House marked a new epoch. Built in 1859, it was the first example of a modern house that in its exterior and interior, in its decoration and furniture, was planned and executed as a single unit. And this happened under sheer necessity: because when the shell of the house was completed, Morris could not find on the market "anything to be bought ready-made that he could be content with in his house: not a chair, or table, or bed; not a cloth or paper hanging for the walls; nor a curtain or a candlestick; nor a jug to hold wine or a glass to drink it out of, but had to be reinvented to escape the flat ugliness of the current article." All furnishings and decoration needed for the house had to be designed by himself and made to order. But when he tried to realize his designs he could not even find a workman able to execute them. All the work of interior decoration was finally done under his own eyes and direction.

A NEW TYPE OF WORKSHOP

The difficulty of furnishing the house when built was one, as Dr. Mackail says, that demanded some more practical solution than that of getting each article singly and laboriously manufactured, even had it been easier than it was to find manufacturers who would accept such orders. There was involved in this difficulty an actual problem, indeed, and its urgency, personally felt and experienced, kindled in Morris the idea of founding his own workshop devoted to producing all sorts of beautiful objects. With some of his friends he established the firm of Morris & Company, the name and wares of which have since become so widely known. "To Morris, who had not yet been forced by business experience into being a business man, the firm probably meant little more than a definite agreement for co-operation and common work among friends who were also artists." The associated members of the firm were the painters Ford Madox Brown and Burne-Jones, both already well-known for their designs for stained glass; Philip Webb, the architect; Faulkner and P. P. Marshall, both engineers by profession.

56

In the first announcement of the firm sent out in 1861, it was stated that the members had felt the want of some one place where work of a genuine and beautiful character might be produced and obtained. Therefore, they had determined to devote their time to designing any species of work susceptible of "art beauty," and like a federation of medieval craftsmen, they had banded themselves together to execute such work by co-operation and at the smallest expense possible. The firm was said to be established for the production of Mural Decoration, Carving, Stained Glass, Furniture and Metal Work. As the main principle of the new firm—and this was the point and something quite new—it was announced that all production was to be done by the members themselves, or under their personal supervision.

At first, the young company was harshly ridiculed and hampered by the intrigues of jealous rivals. But soon, favored by large commissions, it began to flourish. Its products appeared at several exhibitions, and, greatly admired in the circles of the English gentry, soon acquired a wide reputation.

THE POET AS DESIGNER

This was the way that William Morris, the poet, became a decorative manufacturer. Following the principle announced in the first circular of his firm, that nothing should be done in his workshop that he did not know how to do himself, he gradually informed and trained himself in the techniques of the different branches of handicraft: in furniture and textiles, tapestry, ceramics and printing.

His own particular field of work, however, became the designing of flat patterns, especially for all kinds of textiles, for woven stuffs, tapestries and wallpapers. And his ornamental compositions are indeed of a quality unparalleled in the art of the nineteenth century, abnormally fertile though that century was in the production of ornament. For his patterns, Morris frankly follows the medieval style of design: because to him the chief thing was not so much the originality of form as the quality of execution. For his designs, Morris preferred, like his Gothic predecessors, naturalistic motifs taken from the vegetable or animal world and stylized in figures on a large scale. In form and color, all his ornament is founded on careful study of nature. In the designs of his skillful hand, even such an outworn motif as the Acanthus, used over and over again for decorative purposes, acquired a new life and freshness, as may be seen from one of his numerous wallpapers, where he turned this common motif into a powerful ornament rising up like a wave in its rustling rhythm.

As a pattern designer, Morris revealed an imagination as inventive as it was prolific. One of his biographers estimated the total number of his designs for textiles and tapestries at about six hundred. And in all his designs, he revealed a sure understanding of the particular problem of flat pattern: an ornamental composition that covers the ground in an harmonious balance of lines and colors, forming a pleasant but neutral background that carries the eye agreeably along but attracts little attention to itself. Looking at his patterns from a distance, the particular motif fades away, it loses its individual meaning: it becomes a mere arabesque, form without content, a serene interplay of ornamental lines limited only by the rules of strong rhythm. The pattern, thus, enlivens the ground without overcrowding it or, worse, perforating it. In this regard, the designs of William Morris not only attain the quality of their originals, but frequently even excel them. They really reach a degree of perfection comparable to the best examples of Oriental carpets, even to that most characteristic of their attributes: an absolute neutrality of pattern which enables them to harmonize with any style and provides a universal adaptability and perpetual modernity that survives the transient phases of style and fashion. In fact, Morris' designs justify the wide renown that they still retain, and their qualities will be treasured by the taste of every epoch to come.

PRACTICAL RESULTS OF AN IMPRACTICABLE IDEA

William Morris was a poet and an artist, and it was in the cause of art that he became a passionate socialist. As a socialist, he saw the defects and weaknesses of the existing order, and was conscious of the fact that the decay of art was due to the decay of society. As an artist, he plunged into the daring adventure of trying to reform a decaying society by reviving craftsmanship and restoring the dignity and morale of work. To re-establish the Golden Age of craftsmanship, where the worker knew no higher ambition than serviceability, Morris fought against the Iron Age, where the great aim was vendibility and profit. That heroic effort failed. In stating the problem, he misinterpreted the signs of the times; and, we must also admit, the stronger battalions were on the side of his adversaries. But, in aspiring to a new ideal of labor, he met, even in his retrospective manner, a very actual problem, which still remains to be solved.

Moreover, the impracticable ideas of a sensitive artist, aspiring to the unequaled standards of a past perfection, succeeded in bringing about some practical results of greatest importance. With his exemplary achievements in the field of household art, Morris worked wonders in an educational way. Although it has to be admitted that the products of his workshop, made by hand by himself or his fellow-craftsmen, were so expensive that only a select circle of well-to-do amateurs were able to afford them, his work set up a new standard of taste and awakened in the English public a new sensitiveness to truth and genuineness of workmanship. All better new house furniture in England, it has been said, for example, owes something to Webb's experiments done for Morris & Company. It is in this way that Morris finally succeeded in bringing his arch-foe, machine industry, to a pause for self-discipline. Forcing upon industry a new standard of quality in production, his fanatic struggle against the use of the machine mitigated, at the very least, the misuse of that new improved instrument offered by modern technique.

EDUCATIONAL VALUE OF THE GOTHIC PATTERN

The types of Morris' designs, the models of his furniture and the patterns of his tapestries and textiles, as it has been pointed out, were taken from medieval sources. Thus, his work was not in the nature of an original creation. But inspired by the same ideals as were inherent in Gothic art, it was based solidly on the feeling of truth, honesty and naturalness. And to that extent, and for its time, it was original. In the vast flood of a merely formalistic architecture produced in the sixties by the sham Gothic Revival best represented in the extensive work of Sir Gilbert Scott (which produced, as Mr. Kenneth Clark has said, so little on which our eyes can rest without pain), the work of William Morris and his comrades stands out like a green island. To adhere to the Gothic tradition was for Morris not a choice but a following of true mental kinship. And he revealed, indeed, an amazingly positive feeling for modern problems of structure when he said: "We should take Gothic architecture by the hand, and know it for what it was and what it is: a magnificent manifestation of organic order. Proceeding on such a tradition, one avows a principle of structure that evolves its forms in the spirit of strict truthfulness, following the conditions of use, material, and construction."

The principle characterized in this statement gives the key to the modern problem of structure. But in trying to interpret these problems, Morris still needed the image of Gothic architecture; for the age could not think of its problems of building in other than historical form and terms. It is, however, a remarkable fact, and by no means an accident, that all the architects who are found to be forerunners and pioneers of the spirit of modern building were enthusiastic admirers of Gothic art and sworn enemies of Renaissance architecture. On another occasion, Morris said that he found it difficult to put himself in such a frame of mind that he could accept even St. Paul's Cathedral in London as a substitute for even the latest and worst Gothic building! At the same time, in France, Viollet-le-Duc

(1814-1879), a constructive spirit, made an impassioned plea for the adoption of Gothic, the great national tradition of his country, as the basis of architectural education. Its structural principles he exhibited and interpreted in a long series of profound studies, inspired by the same feeling that imbued William Morris: the feeling that in these principles the problems of the new age might be nearer to solution than was possible under the spell of academic classicism. "If we consider," he wrote in the preface to his voluminous *Dictionnaire Raisonné de l'Architecture,* "the study of medieval architecture as useful, and capable of bringing about gradually a happy revolution in art, we must realize that it is not for the purpose of obtaining work without originality or for the indiscriminate reproduction of historical forms; it is, on the contrary, to know the principles which gave rise to these forms: principles which might bear fruit again today, introducing modern ideas conforming to the needs and customs of the present moment."

This statement shows a clear perception of the main basic problem which the spirit of modern building had to deal with. But Viollet-le-Duc stood alone in his country with such prophetic ideas, and his rousing voice was lost in the pathetic rhetoric of the academic classicists. His lectures at the Ecole des Beaux Arts brought upon him the passionate attacks of all the conservatives, and he was finally forced, by the systematic opposition of his pupils, to resign from his chair, which was occupied after him by Hippolyte Taine, the founder of the milieu-theory.

62

NEW DOMESTIC ARCHITECTURE IN ENGLAND

William Morris was not a professional architect, nor did he, according to Dr. Mackail, his biographer, in all his life ever build a house. "But for him, the word architecture always bore an immense, and one might almost say a transcendental meaning. Connected at a thousand points with all the other specific arts which ministered to it out of a thousand sources, it was itself the tangible expression of all the order, the comeliness, the sweetness, nay, even the mystery and the law, which sustain man's world and make human life what it is. To him, the House Beautiful represented the visible form of life itself. Not only as a craftsman and manufacturer, a worker in dyed stuffs and textiles and glass, a pattern designer and decorator, but throughout the whole range of life, he was from first to last the architect, the master-craftsman, unperplexed by artificial subdivisions of art, and untrammeled by any limiting rules of professional customs." The nature of his all-embracing personality cannot be better characterized than in this felicitous statement, and it is by the power of this personality that Morris opened the path for the new spirit of building, far beyond the boundaries of his own land.

Now, to speak first of his native country, the influence of the Arts-and-Crafts movement was not tardy in making itself felt. The example first set by Philip Webb, when he built the Red House, was soon followed on a large scale by two of his contemporaries, by Eden Neshfield and Norman Shaw. Interested in real building rather than in architectural design, they realized that the modern architect, the product of academic education, approached the task of domestic architecture with conceptions much too high to permit an adequate solution of such everyday problems. Looking backward—and backward again because there was as yet no way of attaining insight, except the retrospective method of historical analogy—looking back at the remains of the Queen Anne period, at the simple dwelling houses of the early eighteenth century, built in brick or timber framework, they discovered that this everyday building was much better done by the former master builder and simple craftsman than by the modern type of educated architect. Thus, they abandoned the pretentious use of patterns of monumental architecture for the simple objects of domestic building, and by following the conceptions and customs of the old master-builders, tried, instead, to revive the tradition of indigenous building. Thereby they succeeded in freeing English architecture, stifled with the barren formalism of Neo-Gothic, from the spook of style architecture, and opened up to it the real sources of native tradition, still alive, but buried under the academic sham revival of the national Gothic or its more hideous suburban adaptations.

In the seventies, Norman Shaw became a leading figure in English architecture, and at this time was one of the busiest architects in London. He erected a great many dwelling houses and cottages in and around London, and also built several studios for London artists, delightful little buildings, full of romantic temper and breathing the sublime mood of a lyric poem. On the other hand, he was the first architect who devoted his interest to such a realistic problem as the small house for the middle classes, and he found exemplary solution in his development for Bedford Park, near London, a colony of small houses, erected as single-, double-, and row houses, which produced a great sensation in 1880. In his later years, Norman Shaw recanted and returned to the beatific principles of the classical doctrine. However, it is his historical merit and perhaps his greatest achievement that he, a master planner himself, drew general attention anew to the problem of planning.

This problem was then made the main goal of that school of architects which came in with the next generation, represented by such names as C. R. Ashbee, E. L. Lutyens, C. F. A. Voysey, M. H. Baillie Scott and C. R. Mackintosh, to mention only a few of the leaders. In trying to find a satisfactory solution to this problem, they established anew the principle that the plan must be based upon the organized life within the building. They broke away from the convention of putting the external appearance of the house above the joy of living in it, and, instead, started from the conception of the house as an organism to be developed inside and out as a single unit. Following the old tradition of the manor house and the indigenous dwellings of the peasantry, the work of this new school marked a pronounced tendency towards realism. The increasing desire for livability and the fulfillment of all the functions of the house became the chief aim of planning.

The practical efforts towards such an end are plainly visible in all parts of the plan, in the shape and size of the rooms as well as in their disposition. And in providing for the setting, care is always taken to ensure close connection between house and garden. Thus, these new houses of the so-called "Cottage Style," avoiding the inconveniences and burden of ritual, formerly imposed by an excessive desire for display, were not only intimate and cozy, but expressive of the good life, indoors and out. In their exteriors, they display a new sense for the reality and dignity of the material, resulting in a new honesty and genuineness in its use. For their architectural effect, the houses depend solely on the varied grouping of the masses built closely to the ground, broad-stretched in long horizontal lines and covered with steep roofs of manifold forms. The interiors show the same tendency towards breadth and simplicity, a simplicity often verging on Puritanism: no more furniture than is really needed and that simplified in shape by reduction to basic forms, the plain surface of which is sometimes enlivened, in order to avoid excessive plainness, with the thin tendril lines of Pre-Raphaelite ornament. In this way the English dwelling changed, under the creative efforts of the generation following Morris, to a form that contained, in the germ, the elements of modern domestic building. Therefore, the works of these architects are felt to be thoroughly modern, in spite of the historical reminiscences that still clung about them. And even their excessive tendency towards picturesque effects does not diminish this impression.

Thus, when William Morris died in 1896, at the age of sixty-two, a first and decisive position had been gained for the new spirit of building. One may be surprised that this first important success was achieved in England, a country generally considered very conservative in art, and preferring a conventional but safe solution to the risky experiments of innovation, the final issue of which is always problematic. There is, however, a natural explanation for this surprising fact: England, because of the priority of her progress in industry, was early subjected to the transforming influence of the new economic forces. Thus it was precisely in England that there arose a decisive reaction against the debasing effects of reckless industrialism. And it was a double reaction: one of the reason as well as one of the senses. It was reason that demanded restriction of Manchester's abuses of *laissez-faire,* and its demand inaugurated the great social reform of the forties, with its extensive legislation dealing with pauperism and the improvement of the life of the laborer. And it was the senses, always striving for beauty, that began to rebel against the ugliness of the new industrial world and the desolate features of its new urban districts. A movement for esthetic reform was inaugurated, and although its program for a better life of beauty has not been fulfilled as yet, it succeeded at least in a fundamental reform of domestic building. The British, trained and accustomed to follow the rules of common sense in the practical conduct of life, responded to the change of life with a change of the dwelling, readily accepting the principles of a reform which so obviously, and in all respects, corresponded to the main virtue of the national mind, to the spirit of common sense. Because of her priority in achieving these new ideas of building, England gained at this time considerable influence on the Continent. But it is worth noticing that her advances were strictly limited to the domain of domestic architecture. As a matter of fact, England—apart from the organizing concept of the Garden City—has since made no further contribution to the solution of the multiplying problems which from then on engross the modern spirit of building.

PART TWO

THE LIBERATION FROM
HISTORICAL FORMS

1. THE ROLE OF THE ENGINEERS

THE LINE OF CREATIVE BUILDING

Tracing the line of creative building through the course of the nineteenth century, we will find it keeping aloof from the precincts of high architecture and taking its direction strictly among utilitarian buildings. In fact, the great achievements of the century in building, the works of historical significance, originated from the disciplined mind of the engineers rather than from the roving fancy of the architects. It is not the architecture of our modern city halls, libraries, and museums, designed for monumental display rather than for practical use, that first manifested the new spirit of building, but it is the new iron bridges and derricks, the furnaces and cooling towers, the silos and wide-spanned worksheds, in short the works of the engineers which wholly changed the face of the cultivated land. While architecture at this time was in general reactionary in its attitude and reminiscent in its effect, and even the best works of the leading academic masters revealed but vestigial ideas, the works of the engineers appeared as buildings of a really creative nature, announcing something new and pointing towards the future. In these impressive structures, a world of new forms was opened up, forms as new in their nature as they were strong and exciting in their effect.

71

ENGINEERING: A NEW PROFESSION

As a special profession, engineering came into being with the use of new materials, such as iron and glass, offered by the progress of Technique: materials heretofore either unknown or, at least, not utilized for building purposes in the same scale and manner. A special expert was needed to develop new methods of construction, adapted to the nature and the physical properties of these building materials. In order to base these methods on the firm ground of science, affording the security of exact calculation with the advantages of greatest economy, a new scientific branch was developed: Statics, a mathematical discipline, requiring a good deal of theoretical knowledge heretofore not needed in the practice of building.

Thus, in full accordance with the principle of division of labor, which dominates the modern process of production, specialization took place in the building profession, too, dividing it into two different fields, artistic and constructive—and that to its great detriment.

Specialization in building set in pretty early. It began with the development of military architecture, when the rise of long-range guns made necessary a new art of fortification requiring special experts. It was then definitely established in France, the country of reason, where the art of engineering, after Italy's early lead, came to its fullest development. With the foundation of the Ecole des Ponts et Chaussées in Paris, in 1747, road building and hydraulic engineering became a special domain separated from the activities of the "architecte decoratif" and entrusted to a particularly trained expert, the "architecte constructeur," who later on was called an engineer. With the new tasks coming in with the nineteenth century, his domain was considerably enlarged, and it is the engineer who finally came to deal with all modern, that is to say, really vital building problems. The architect, on the other hand, became a specialist, too, as already revealed in his new name, a professional designer of decoration, at once magnifying and trivializing his job by borrowing historical details, by using ready-made ornaments and by contriving ever-new variations of the perennial five orders of columns.

There are many examples illustrating the different methods of procedure followed by the engineer and the architect. Many a modern bridge of iron construction, for instance, demands recognition as an outstanding achievement on the part of the engineer who strictly followed the stern command of use, and out of the conditions of the material and the construction derived the form. This form, often very impressive in the rapid flow of its lines and the powerful effect of its contours, is then impaired by the architect, who, following his ideology of decoration, attempts to embellish the naked structure by building up monumental pillars and gates draped with historical forms taken over, for instance, from the tower of a medieval castle.

ON THE NATURE OF TECHNICAL FORM

At a time when the architects voluntarily restricted themselves to the esthetic problems of building, busy about solving them in the spirit of the academic doctrine, the engineers took in hand the new problems of construction and developed, in the way of methodical research and tedious experiment, both the theoretical and practical foundations of modern building. While the architects, devoted only to the formalistic problems of style, became more and more estranged from the fundamentals of their art, the engineers remained in close contact with their time and kept pace with the practice of building. Thereby they rendered an eminent service to architecture. Their notable mission consisted in conserving the principles of real creative building at a time when architecture, fatally misguided by its one-sided esthetic point of view, drove at full speed to catastrophe. With the results of their work, which proved to have a strong sensuous effect, though they did not follow the academic doctrine at all, the engineers propagated the moral demand to keep away from esthetics and to deal, first of all, with the technical problems of building and the demands of use. It was due to the educational influence springing from the works of the engineers that the architect's attention, as yet one-sidedly concentrated on the form alone, the final result of artistic creation, was gradually turned again to the way to form, to the process of creating the form.

All technical form is pure form of use. From the first tools, from hammer and plow, up to the modern dynamo turbine, all technical form was developed solely out of the function the object had to serve. And the history of the technical form is but a continuous process of refining the form by more and more adapting it to its function. Step by step, advancing from experiment to experiment, the form is materialized, extricated and pulled out of the matter and gradually developed into its final state in

74

a long process of adapting the object to the demand of its use, to the nature of the material and to the instrument employed in the process of production. The technical form is not invented on the drawing board through the efforts of the individual designer, but developed in practice in a process of collective effort, and it is on that account that Lewis Mumford calls engineering the most impersonal of the arts. As in horticulture a new species of plant or flower is produced by means of crossing and cultivation, so in technique the way to create a new form is by a process of breeding carried through a long series of tedious experiments. And this process of cultivation and refinement, kept in motion by collective efforts, is not ended until the pure form of use is obtained, a form satisfying the demands of highest efficiency. In this way all our modern machinery, our ships and locomotives, our automobiles and airplanes, found the final forms we now so highly admire for their perfection. In the rise of these forms of modern technique, a process of morphological evolution has passed before our eyes. In every single stage this persistent impulse towards highest efficiency has enhanced the purity of the form.

In these products of modern technique, in the works of the engineers, architecture was given a new orientation, not from an esthetic point of view, it goes without saying, but from the point of view of structure: as pure form of use, adapted to a certain function, all technical form is organic in character; and so by its nature it demonstrates the basic principle of order that the new spirit of building is pursuing.

2. ART NOUVEAU:
RISE OF A NEW ORNAMENT

Up to the time of William Morris' death, all attempts to realize a new spirit of building had been made by linking up with the past. Its disciples not only envisaged their problems by historic analogy, but also took over the language of the historical architecture in which to express that spirit. Towards the end of the nineteenth century came the first liberation from the bondage of historical styles and style ideas. This new phase of the movement was enacted on the Continent, and began its fermentation especially in northern Europe, with Germany well in the lead. The new creative impulse grew out of the experience with the new forms evolved by modern technique. They gave, as we have seen, a new meaning to the problem of structure and to the entire scene a new aliveness.

Let us take a glimpse at the esthetic temper of the moment. In 1889, as a widely visible landmark for the World's Exposition in Paris, the French engineer, Gustave Eiffel, erected the great iron tower that soared from its foundations in daring sweeping curves and reached the hitherto unattained building height of about 1000 feet: the first real "skyscraper," and also the most logical one. An early work of engineering, a rather primitive iron construction from the point of view of today. A tight structure of girders and beams, made in rolling mills, impossible to conceive without the background of Modern Industry and mechanized processes of production. *A monument of the iron age, deliberately erected by that age to its own greater glory, and for no other purpose than to proclaim its new constructive power and genius.*

The effect of this powerful demonstration was rather disrupting. Confronted by this audacious yet masterly evidence of a new courage in structural engineering, men of the most honest feelings came to a parting of the ways. The older generation was shocked. They looked with unconcealed contempt at the strange tower. They felt it to be simply ugly. With an indignation that bespoke their inability to see any meaning in the unusual form, they protested with all the fervor of their outraged convictions, in the name of good taste, and of art and its irreplaceable values, "against the vandalism of industrial enterprise," to speak in their own words, against the debasing effects "of this monstrous column of riveted plates, throwing its spidery shadows, like a blot of ink, over the glowing beauty of Paris. . . . All our great monuments, humiliated and reduced in size, will disappear in this stupefying dream. Is the city of Paris going to associate herself any longer with the baroque, mercantile fancies of a builder of machines to the end of irreparably uglifying and dishonoring herself?" Among those who signed the flaming "Protestation des Artistes," one finds the names of the most famous celebrities of the day, such as Victorien Sardou, Alexandre Dumas, François Coppée and Guy de Maupassant, to mention but a few, and all of them belonged to the same generation as Ruskin and Morris.

The new generation was enchanted. Full of admiring approval, it stood before this thrilling spectacle and accepted it as a revelation of the form of its own age. It felt simply overwhelmed with the new beauty. Its conviction was eloquently expressed by Henry van de Velde, who in the further course of the movement was soon to ascend to the rôle of a leader. "There is a class of men," he announced in one of his first manifestoes, "from whom we cannot withhold the title of artist. Their work rests, first, on the use of materials hitherto unknown to building; and secondly, on a boldness so startling that it surpasses that of the great cathedral builders. These artists, the creators of a new architecture, are the engineers. The soul of their work is Reason. The means is Calculation. The consequence of their use of reason and calculation may be the surest and purest beauty."

We will attach no more importance to these emphatic words than is due to a rhetorical exaggeration. But from them we may measure the degree of enthusiasm awakened in the younger generation, as it looked at the works of the engineers and felt the stimulating and arousing effect of these new creations. Whether or no we call the engineer an artist, he is certainly a builder, a constructor, and therefore he is an inexorable realist. Close to reality, his method of procedure is directed straightforwardly towards the exact fulfillment of the demand for efficiency, and in adapting his structure to this end, he develops the form that best suits the purpose. "The works of modern technique," said van de Velde, praising their sensuous effects, "teach us that it is an error to search for beauty in any other forms than in those best suited to their purpose."

THE SEARCH FOR A GUIDING PRINCIPLE

When, in the early nineties, the generation of Henry van de Velde pushed forward into the *Art Nouveau* Movement, it was the previous reform movement in England and the successful experiments in a new realistic architecture essayed by William Morris' followers, in the domain of domestic building, from which they took their ideas and drew their inspiration. At about this time in Germany another experiment toward such a realistic architecture was made by Alfred Messel, when he built the Wertheim's Department Store in 1896. In this case efficiency demanded a light-flooded interior, so the architect dissolved the enclosing walls into a system of vertical granite piers, and filled the wide intervals with great areas of glass. This building still contained some reminiscences of historical forms, and the old-fashioned roof of French descent certainly does not agree with the modern system of piers. Yet the design on the whole manifested a strong feeling for reality. By its undaunted realism it gained great influence among the young generation, giving a fresh impetus to the new spirit of building.

To think realistically and be guided by the demand of use and purpose became to the young generation an obligation as sacred as it was self-evident. Yet not thus could they realize the further goal of innovation set up by their youthful self-confidence. They longed for their own language of form. They wanted to be rid of historical style concepts and to find an elementary form that belonged to their own time. To overcome the complete anarchy of form they found themselves living in, an anarchy brought about by the indiscriminate use of old styles and the thoughtless copying of their forms, they realized that the movement first needed the rigid guidance of a principle of structure, a principle of general validity by which creative instinct would be bound and directed anew. In seeking such a guiding principle that could help to interpret the actual problem of structure, their predecessors, as we have seen, returned to Gothic art. To them, such a guiding principle was inherent in the creations of modern technique, the only works of the time that revealed not only a style of complete unity, but one in which there was also a novel beauty. This guiding principle, followed by modern technique, was defined by Henry van de Velde in terms of "logical conception" and "reasonable beauty." And intrigued by its generative force, on it he based the idea of a new style.

SOCIOLOGICAL GROUNDWORK

If the definition of the principle was rather vague and debatable, the tendency of the new belief was clearly revealed, when van de Velde said that a thing can be shaped into a form that corresponds to its nature and natural law, only when the process of production is developed according to reason. When van de Velde, in a terminology of his own, talked about a principle of "logical conception" and "reasonable beauty," he was really endeavoring to interpret with this somewhat rationalistically colored phrase the structural problem of the pure form of use. He was groping for a definition of the principle of organic order.

This becomes manifest in one of his later writings. He explains at greater length the leading idea of his theory, when he discusses the structural character of the styles. And he contrasts the organic styles which he calls "the styles of the great tribes," with the styles of the Renaissance and its descendants, the Baroque and Rococo, which, as he says, divorced the idea of beauty from that of purpose, deliberately failing to recognize the function of what had once been organic.

As a matter of fact, with his theory, which was less concerned with esthetic problems or with a doctrine of beauty than with the problem of structure itself, van de Velde developed a new morphology, the basic principle of which was a clear response to the demand for organic order. And the progress of the new spirit of building in knowing and penetrating its problem, is revealed in the fact that van de Velde did not seek a justification for his doctrine in the domain of esthetics alone. He achieved a sociological basis for his theory, arguing that it is the principle of organic structure that determines the thought of our time and acts as the guiding idea in the process in which all phases of society and economy are being transformed. To follow this principle, van de Velde declared, means to include, in the guiding ideas of the day, the method of producing the form; means to bring all artistic production in accord with the spirit, the manners and morale of the new epoch; means, therefore, setting the feet anew on the fostering soil on which alone can grow a unified style of the time.

In this well-founded doctrine in which the principle of the new building is oriented to a fundamental sociological synthesis, Henry van de Velde prepared the theoretical groundwork for the revolutionary movement to which the power of his enthusiasm had given the impulse. The *Art Nouveau* movement, starting in Belgium, gained ground rapidly in Germany, and from there spread throughout northern Europe. Van de Velde gathered about him the most independent and forceful talents of the time; men like Hermann Obrist, August Endell, Bernhard Pankok, Richard Riemerschmid, Otto Eckmann and Peter Behrens joined the advance guard of the movement. All of them had been painters, and they were in rebellion against the social isolation to which their studio methods condemned them. They crowded forward to another and wider field of activity that brought them in closer contact with community life and made them what the artist once had been and ought to be: a true and indispensable member of society. It is always the same: the artist, in the fundamentals of his working existence closely connected with the fate of society, suffers most from its unsettled conditions. Thus, he feels in himself the moral summons to collaborate in social reform, and in this way he gets the first consciousness of the real artistic problems of his time.

CREATING A NEW ORNAMENT

In the first attack, the little band poured out its energy with revolutionary ardor, and battled onward to its high goal. And once again we see a splendid courage spending itself against a totally unprepared society. The valorous but thin line of artists

ART NOUVEAU

Interior, 1896. Designed by **G. Serrurier-Bovy**

Interior (study), 1903. Designed by Henry van de Velde

Interior (music room). Designed by M. H. Baillie Scott at Mannheim, Germany

THE GARTH, England. M. A. Baillie Scott, architect

THE RED HOUSE, England, 1859. William Morris and Philip Webb, architects

was powerless to change the methods by which society went about its building. Baffled by the resistance of established foundations, they plunged into an attack on that part easiest of access but least essential to the whole: ornament. Spurning the historical manner of decoration, they invented a new one.

The history of art proves, however, that the advent of a new style is always announced first in a change of decoration. Because it is difficult to change the structure of building without altering economic and social relations a new impetus first becomes visible in the agile and easily changeable art of decoration. Here the artist occupies himself with covering the surface of furniture and all small objects of use with fresh ornamental forms that manifest the new direction of the imagination. And so it was in the history of modern building. With the rise of the *Art Nouveau* movement, a fresh start was made with the invention of a new ornament. And to begin with the beginning, the young revolutionists first designed a new type for printing—and, artists as they were, every one of them invented his own personal type. From type they went on to invent new patterns for tapestries and textiles. They gradually turned to furniture and house furnishing and the decoration of individual rooms; and then pushing on to form the dwelling as a whole, they finally arrived at the essential problems of building.

Throughout the whole movement plenty of new forms were invented, but taken together they show no unity. And in its whole development the movement practically never got beyond the stage of creating ornaments. The great hopes based on the invention of a new ornament show their exalted belief in the spiritual significance of ornament itself. For them, the ornament was considered as much a channel for self-expression as any other kind of human art activity. From this high appreciation resulted their sincere indignation against such ordinary and meaningless decoration as that which covers the whole surface with insignificant compositions of flowers, fruits and naked women. This debased ornament, degenerated by an excess of naturalism, they tried to replace by spiritual and symbolic ornament based on the psychic expressiveness of the lines. They visualized an abstract ornament with dramatic qualities, revealing in its structure the whole scale of human sentiment and feelings, such as gladness and grief, weariness and force, etc. And they wanted this ornament no longer applied to its object, but arising from it, indicating its purpose, its material and construction and also the process of its production: in other words, they wanted an ornament that could be thought of as being an organ, expressing in the dynamic lines of its structure the different functions of resting and supporting, of bending and tension, of hanging, gripping, suspending, and so on. And with that new type of organic ornament they wanted to replace the historical form elements, the classic columns and capitals, the cornices and moldings, used ready-made until now.

GOTTFRIED SEMPER

Such ideas were not quite new. Let it be remembered that similar definitions had been used and discussed about two generations ago by the German architect Gottfried Semper (1803-1879) . He spoke of "a constructive, or better dynamic principle

84

of ornamentation," and he demanded that each part of a work as well as its whole should manifest what it has to do, in other words should express its function; and this not only by its form, but also in its ornament. Regretting the lack of a book teaching the principles of style in their adaptation to the new inventions of science and manufacture, he devoted a good part of his life to studies aimed to fill that gap, and in 1860-1863 published a comprehensive work of two volumes, entitled *Der Stil in den technischen und tektonischen Künsten.*

This illuminative book, revealing the mind of a profound thinker, takes as its main object the problem of structure. Dealing with it from a genetic point of view, exploring the origin of the form in architecture and decoration, the author explains the structure as derived from the nature of the material, the method of construction and the purpose of use; and following this interpretation, he established the theory that all structure is determined by these three conditions. The structure, however, according to his theory, is covered with a texture of artistic forms; a conclusion plainly manifesting that he still misunderstood the close relation between structure and form, which represents an integral unity, the form being developed out of the structure rather than added to it as a special artistic element. No wonder, then, that as an architect Semper adopted precisely the Renaissance pattern as best apt to supply the formal texture to his designs, among which the Opera House in Dresden (destroyed by fire in 1869) and his great town-planning schemes for Vienna were the most significant.

As a philosopher, Semper followed, as one can see from the

mechanistic nature of his theory, the contemporary mode of thinking, a mode largely influenced by Darwin's theory of evolution. Semper's interpretation of the problem of structure, however, greatly stimulated the movement in its advance towards a theory, something always needed before a new practice can be developed. Gaining a large influence with the following generation, it became the keyword for the *Art Nouveau* movement, and its leader, Henry van de Velde, cites Gottfried Semper's name beside those of William Morris and Viollet-le-Duc among the men whose influence helped him to develop his theory of a new style.

"YACHTING STYLE"

It is in the work of van de Velde himself that we may observe the nature of this new style in its purest and most unrestrained form. He is the real initiator as well as the most original inventor of that abstract and spiritual ornament which gave the *Art Nouveau* movement its particular character, and which was soon discredited by the inferior works of unscrupulous imitators. There is no better way to describe the nature of this style and to characterize the principle of structure on which it is based than by quoting van de Velde's laconic statement: "The line is a force." A new path of self-expression was revealed in these ornamental lines overloaded with symbolism. That this ornament grew out of painting is to be seen from the early designs of van de Velde, flat patterns for rugs and woven stuffs, patterns which obviously poured from a brush, not from a pencil. What van Gogh, the painter, achieved with the dramatic force of his brush-

86

strokes, van de Velde sought in the expressive lines of his abstract ornament. With it, there were already realized certain ideas which more recently have dominated the school of abstract painting.

Starting as a painter and from ornament and proceeding self-taught to building, van de Velde, the architect, developed an individualistic style which reveals unmistakably in every detail his characteristic handwriting. The tendency towards abstraction which kept his mind in subjection, made him prefer plain and smooth forms of various moldings, such as are to be seen in the decoration for the entrance hall of the Weimar Museum, and in the architecture of the little theater which he built in the name of the Deutsche Werkbund for the Exposition at Cologne in 1914. Looking at this individualistic example of functionalism, one may be disposed to take it as an effective anticipation of the streamline theory rather than as an experiment in modern dynamic architecture. It is from this preference for curved lines that the Brothers Goncourt characterized his manner as the "Yachting Style."

SENTIMENT VERSUS REASON

When van de Velde's attention was once called to the fact that his furniture was constructed in open conflict with the nature of the material, he bluntly declared to the objector that for a long time he had been convinced of the inadequacy of wood as material for his designs, and that he anticipated the discovery of a more suitable material which could be cast: a remark that seemed to foresee the invention of the steel chair of today.

However, there was lying in wait a conflict between the command of reason, at first proclaimed as the guiding principle of the movement, and the exuberant urge to expression that poured itself out in the forms and decorations of the *Art Nouveau*. So strong was the intensity of the urge that all craft traditions and technical rules, all laws of material and construction, even the most obvious demands of use and purpose, were cast aside. That first fine consecration to the logic of a reasonable concept was completely forgotten. The rational doctrine with which the movement began, based as it was on the controlling power of reason, was offset, in the result, by a world of irrational forms that merely reflected the uncontrollable urge to express. Sentiment became once more victorious over reason. The theory of the movement fell a victim to the wayward willfulness of fantasy. The youthful band took the field to seek and to find the eternal style of the pure form of use, but they became mired in the ornamental—not in the pure form flowing from "the logical conception," but the abstract form of sentimental expression. They aspired to the typical, to the form of universal validity, and they came to an end in a complete subjectivism!

This fatal failure to reconcile theory and practice, which does not in any way diminish the esthetic originality of the new forms created in the course of the movement, is forcibly illustrated in a fine episode told by Gotthard Jedlicka in his book on Toulouse-Lautrec. In 1894, van de Velde built himself a small house in Uccle near Brussels. Down to the last detail it was intended to demonstrate his own ideas. To it, one day, came Toulouse-Lautrec and Joynant his friend and biographer. The guests, after having inspected the house, were charmed with their impressions. Nothing had been left to chance: the library was really a place to study in, the nursery, painted in white, was joyous. The hostess' gown harmonized beautifully with the dining room and the colored glasses on the table. The colors of the plates, even of the food in the dishes were but single parts of an ensemble. The tendency towards harmony, as Joynant diffidently remarked was rather too distinctly felt. They were perplexed with the play of *valeurs* covering the table cloth; lit up by the sun, the grating of the windows cast its shadow on the floor; the light, falling through the stained-glass window panes, split the room in layers of various colors. Yellow eggs and red beans were served on china, tinted in green and violet. Joynant, a gourmet, later remarked cynically that it all seemed to have been done at the expense of the cooking. The guests said farewells. On the way home, their opinions, as they reflected on their impressions, underwent a change. "Well," said Toulouse-Lautrec at last, "the only successes are the bathroom, the nursery, painted with white enamel, and the W. C."

In that story, all is told. The sharp criticism that lay in the gentle irony hit not only this single attempt but the whole movement. The new faith was unable to prevent a temporary relapse into the old manners of individualism which were at odds with the theory. In practice, all structure, even the objects of pure use, were interpreted as "objets d'art" and treated as vehicles for a personal artistic expression, and the style they had set out to find appeared only in those anonymous forms that grew out of an impersonal technique.

In its standard works, the new style produced a long series of such typical "objets d'art." Unique performances, of high artistic value, did appear, remarkable achievements because of the individual creative genius, manifesting unbounded force of fantasy, though often more intellectual than instinctive, and a vital will to form, struggling for expression. But the elemental urge to expression, revealing itself as so self-conscious and so self-important in these creations, diminished their value for practical use. And so far removed are these individualistic creations already from our present point of view that, seen in historical perspective, we can appreciate them merely as museum pieces. Exhibited as such in collections of decorative art, they will reveal to the future the unique spirit of this extravagant world of expressive forms that dominated the turn of the century. To those who have lived through this epoch, its particular flavor sometimes comes back in certain pictures of Paul Gauguin, for instance, which appear as strange as they are outmoded, their background filled with an ornamental fabric of symbolic lines and unsound, almost overheated colors.

In the history of modern building, the period of the *Art Nouveau,* or *"Jugendstil"* as it was known in Germany, remains only an episode. It was a courageous experiment looking towards the future, as estimable as the result was dubious. But the fate of evanescence destined to its creations did not diminish the vital power of the doctrine. Its continued influence is proved in the practical results that followed the enlightenment provided by van de Velde and his comrades. It is the lasting merit of van de Velde that he first saw and rightly formulated an actual problem of the time. Disclosing its relation to the driving forces and guiding ideas of the time, he removed the discussion from the limited domain of esthetics and put it under the wide aspect of a new comprehensive culture. The ideal itself has a generative force, and it matters but little how long the practical results of this ideal remain unrealized. When van de Velde and his followers attacked the problem from above, beginning with the outside and demonstrating the new ideas in the form of a new ornament, they were forced to do so by the unsettled conditions of the time, which was still not ripe for accepting the full change of structure in building itself.

"There was a moment in the history of the movement," van de Velde once said, "when our task was revealed to us. At that moment, we freed the objects of our surroundings from all ornament, and began to expose their joints and skeletons, in order to permeate ourselves with the logic of these elementary forms." It is by returning to this task asking for the purification of form that the movement found its way out again of the blind alley where it had become stuck with its emotional adventure of creating an expressive ornament.

A NEW ESTHETIC PURGE

Up to this time, the leaders of the revolutionary movement had been mostly painters who entered the new field of their wider activity self-taught. It was about the turn of the century that the professional architects of Europe, attracted by the idea of a new style and inspired by the results of the *Art Nouveau* movement, began to settle their final accounts with an eclectic architecture founded on the close imitation or zealous adaptation of historical styles.

The professionals opened their attack with an esthetic purge, more concerned with the form and the attendant problem of expression than with the constituent problem of structure. To overcome the multitude of forms conjured up by modern eclecticism, they began to purify the building, thereby restoring its basic structure. With this process of simplification they certainly succeeded in strengthening the emotional effect of the form, but failed to touch the problem of structure. With the theory stated by the *Art Nouveau* movement, this problem had been most strictly defined as a problem of organic order. This problem, however, was not solved by a process of mere purification. The structure itself had not yet been changed. And as this structure was based on the principles of geometric order, it remained the same after the purification of the building from all ornamental details.

To be sure, this tendency towards purification sprang from a desire for formal discipline rather than from evolutionary impulse, and thus it was more reformative than creative in its character. This new tendency of the movement towards purifying the form by reducing it to its geometric stem, has an interesting parallel in the architecture of the second half of the eighteenth century. When, at the end of the Baroque period, as a result of its exuberant urge to expression, the form became more and more dissolved, a rationalistic movement was started in France, promoting a new conception of architecture based again on reason. The leading ideas of the movement are demonstrated in the work of Claude-Nicolas Ledoux (1732-1806). Reducing in its numerous projects the form to the prime elements of Geometry, to the square, the circle and the triangle, he restored the basic ground of all architecture. And from the simple, almost heroic monumentality of the pure bodies of Geometry, his buildings derive a strong emotional appeal. In a recent study devoted to his work, Ledoux has been called a predecessor of Le Corbusier, and indeed, in his conceptions he anticipated the basic ideas of the later architect who by the offerings of modern technique was able to cast his geometric ideas in the form of a graceful modernism.

By taking recourse on their own impulse to the remedy put to test in the work of Ledoux, not knowing anything about him, probably not even his name, the purifiers of the beginning twentieth century helped to restore the feeling for form, ruined by the excesses of academic historicism. And after all, to this process of purification was joined a new tendency toward honesty and truthfulness, shown in construction as well as in the use of material.

DUTCH AND AUSTRIAN CONTRIBUTIONS

This line was first resumed in Holland, with the work of H. P. Berlage. Born in 1857, he became a student of the Zurich Polytechnicum, where at the time Gottfried Semper was one of the foremost teachers. In his beginnings, Berlage was still entangled in the ideas of historical style architecture, as is to be seen from one of his early designs, a project for a mausoleum (1889), perhaps the most intricate instance of nineteenth-century formalism in architecture. But soon he saw the sterility of this kind of form concept, and with strong self-discipline tried to find his way back to a more fundamental basis for the evolution of form. He developed his own concept which in its essence turns out to be an unreserved return to the geometric principles of structure: he based his designs on a network of squares, and into that scheme the various parts of the plan as well as of the façade were divided, according to the law of geometrical proportions. He expounded his theory in a little essay, *Ideas on Style in Architecture,* published in 1905. But following this theory on a rationalistic basis, recognizing the singularity of modern life, responding to its particular demands, and allowing the claims of modern technique, he finally succeeded in developing an architecture which, freed from historical forms, for the first time really appeared as a product of its own period. The new freshness and originality of his work is best to be judged from such a building as the Amsterdam Bourse, finished in 1903; a building as effective in the use of the small-sized Dutch brick and the technical treatment of this attractive material, as excellent in the grouping of the masses. The setting, with the square-built tower on one corner, formed a fine terminal vista for several points of view. In the interior the construction is frankly revealed: in the great hall the large girders are exposed without any applied ornament, contrasting in their dynamic lines with the fine masonry surface of the brick walls. Berlage's form is as frugal as the ornament of the *Art Nouveau* was exuberant, and his puritanism gave his work a stern character of sobriety. But his urge to puritanism was no less intense and genuine than the emotions of the *Art Nouveau* decorators. And his practical example, in its essence more educational than creative, opened a new path for the younger generation.

In Austria, the first impetus to the regeneration was given by Otto Wagner, also a man of the older generation (1841-1918), and a pupil of Gottfried Semper's. In one of his first manifestoes, he stated his belief that "there is no other starting point for our work than modern life." But when it came to work, he did not live up to this profession, and instead of applying the constitutive principles of modern life to the problem of structure, he used in practice, as his starting point, the approved principles of geometric order. He tried to restore the integrity of architecture by reducing the bulk of the building to plain contours and pure form, to simple cubes. By removing all architectural and ornamental relief he freed the façades from historical detail, and covered the surface of the building with thin marble slabs, which gave the walls, with their few joints, a rather modern appearance. Otto Wagner designed the architecture for the Stadtbahn and he also did quite a number of public buildings in Vienna, among them the church for the Steinhof Hospital, a building which clearly reveals how close he still remained to the classical notion of structure. He gained great influence over the younger generation not so much by his work as by his teachings, inspiring his students through the intrepid and unrestricted acknowledgment of the demands of modern life. Among the numerous disciples of the Wagner school, Josef Hoffman was one of the most gifted architects. In the Maison Stoclet, built in 1911 in Brussels, he developed the new technique of surface treatment to such perfection that the house, though in its plan and structure based on the geometrical concept, comes close, at least in its outer appearance, to certain more authentic examples of modern building.

At the same time, Adolf Loos began to disturb the equanimity of the Viennese by his provocative articles and lectures on misuse and misunderstandings in the arts. He certainly was an exceptional figure, a man of varied acquirements, and very gifted in all of them. As a youngster, he came to the United States, where he lived for three years, working his way as a mason, and at other times as a sawyer in a factory for inlaid floors. In this country he saw some machine-made products that impressed him very much by the simple beauty of their plain forms: such articles, for instance, as modern trunks, desk chairs and other standardized office furniture. Later on he settled in Vienna, was an architect by profession, and became a philosopher and reformer of life by circumstances.

Reacting to the undergoing changes of life with an extraordinary sensibility, visualizing the driving forces of the historical development, and never afraid of drawing the necessary conclusions from his observation, Loos began a passionate struggle for a new integrity of life and purity of life conduct. For purity's sake he resisted the ornament on a plate as he disapproved of the flour in the spinach served on this plate. As the only possible pattern for the industrial age he advocated the pure form of use, based on that theory of "logical conception," established by van de Velde, but in practice so disgracefully betrayed and abandoned when the movement glided back into ornamental ecstasy. Ornament roused all his passions, and to such an extent that he once flung from the table of his café in Vienna the sharply pointed remark: "Ornament is a crime," an aphorism which for a long time became the popular slogan of the movement, used *pour épater le bourgeois*. The essence of Loos' conviction is expressed in his statement that marks the line along which the modern spirit of building developed: "The evolution of culture is identical with the abandonment of ornament in the objects of use." In all his buildings and interior decorations he strongly lived up to his conviction. In their simple forms and their abstinence from any ornament, they disclosed a character, felt at this time as an exhibit of radical modernism—as proved by the fact that the completion of one of his buildings in Vienna was temporarily prohibited by the building authorities.

NEW INDUSTRIAL BUILDING

There was probably no other country in Europe, where the influence of the *Art Nouveau* movement was more strongly felt than in Germany. Impressed by the lofty aim of van de Velde's program and inspired by his all-embracing theory, the new spirit of building gained momentum, and, rapidly spreading among the younger architects, soon conquered now domains. The change of conception was first seen in the field of industrial building. And it is certainly not by accident that this new spirit first came to act on such utilitarian buildings as factories, office buildings, department stores, worksheds and storage houses. To solve the problems involved in these new types of building, a strict rationality was needed, and strong technical logic. It is in the nature of the problem that its solution has to be sought in a realistic conception, truly devoted to the demands for service and efficiency, and conscientiously utilizing the means of modern technique, the new processes of production as well as modern materials and construction. And as the stern command of use is even sterner and almost inexorable, as far as the claims for economy are concerned, there is no chance in this type of building for architectural display, for showy forms and sumptuous decoration. By the force of this rigid necessity, the architects, restrained to the demands of use and purpose alone, came to an initial understanding of the technical and economic problems of modern building. In this way, industrial building became the experimental field, where the problem of structure was first thought of and practiced anew, with the result that new forms were produced, no longer derived from historical patterns; forms as strange and unusual in their aspect as strong and impressive in their effect.

Perhaps the most interesting original examples of this new development are to be found in the work of Hans Poelzig. In his younger years he erected a series of industrial buildings, in which the new structural problems are not only realized but already solved in a form fresh and full of strength and sap, and not reached again by later followers of the movement. And this impressive form is always developed from the practical demands of use alone, from the conditions of material and construction. In the effective grouping of the masses, in the design of the contours, in the treatment of the walls and roofs, these buildings prove the hand of a real architect. It is to be regretted that this great talent which people expected to push the banners

WATERTOWER
Posen, 1912. Hans
Poelzig, architect

CHEMICAL WORKS
Luban, 1912. Hans
Poelzig, architect

FACTORY BUILDING, Cologne, 1914. Designed for the
German Werkbund Exhibition. Walter Gropius, architect

FACTORY BUILDING, Alfeld, 1914. Walter Gropius, architect

of the movement a good stretch forward, soon got involved in an extreme subjectivism. Misguided by the urgings of his fantasy, Poelzig in his later years developed a style of his own, and, trying to express the universal in these esoteric individual forms, he soon lost contact with the age. As creative expressions of a great architectural temperament, these later projects are still interesting, but the high swing of the fantasy is not always able to compensate for the alienation of the work from the spirit of the age.

To do justice, it is necessary to say, and this will probably surprise the reader, that it was the example of America that gave decisive impulse to the German architects when they first tried to clarify the problem of structure. To be sure, this impulse did not originate, as one might be inclined to assume, in the skyscraper, which this country likes to claim as its quite original invention. On the contrary, this new type of building, at this time still in a primitive state and exhibiting an extreme formalism, mixed of reminiscences of all historical styles, was cited as an example illuminating how the pressure of conventional conceptions might obstruct the plain solution of a modern building problem. Not these pretentious office buildings were the examples that attracted the attention of the German architects, but the simple structures of industrial building, such as the grain-elevators and big silos to be found in the great grain ports all over South America. These examples of modern engineering, designed for practical use only, and obviously without any decorative assistance from an architect, made a deep impression by their simple structure reduced to basic forms of geometry, such as cubes and cylinders. They were conceived as patterns exemplifying once more the essence of the pure form of use, gaining its impressive effect from its bare structure.

The influence spreading from this pattern was soon apparent, and indeed was sometimes so strong as to lead to mere imitation, as shown, for instance, in such a building as the water tower and gas tank for the gas works in Frankfort on the Main, erected by Peter Behrens in 1912. In this design, as in those of many other buildings, Behrens—at this time one of the most accomplished specialists in industrial building—proved himself a pioneer in restoring architectural law, subjecting the problem of design to the discipline of geometric form. It is due to that inclination that he succeeded in filling his form with monumental sentiment, raising it to ostentatious effect. So strict and fervent was his endeavor to achieve a generalization of form that he almost appears as the academician of the movement.

Once more, however, it has to be emphasized that the problem of form is one thing, and the problem of structure is another. The first is an esthetic problem only, and the other is decidedly a morphological one. The two problems are of a different character, and as the history of the movement proves, they have not always been clearly distinguished, not even in the present day. Discussing the basic problem of structure, and aiming at the pure form of use, the movement, over and over again entangled in esthetic problems, contented itself with the esthetic satisfaction derived from the pure forms of geometry.

THE DEUTSCHE WERKBUND

To sum up: the *Art Nouveau* movement did not succeed in fulfilling its ambitious program endeavoring no less than the creation of a new style. But it succeeded in loosening the minds and spreading the new spirit over wider regions. And there is perhaps no better example to prove the educational influence of the movement than the organization that grew out of it in Germany, well known under the name of *Deutsche Werkbund*. It was founded by artists devoted to the emerging ideas of the movement. It was felt that the new art needed a social soil to take root and to grow in. To prepare such a fostering soil, they appealed to industry, as the most advanced constituent of economic organization, admonishing it to become conscious of the cultural responsibility that devolved upon it with its leading rôle in modern society. With the assistance of and in co-operation with industrial enterprise, it was assumed, the movement would be able to define and focus the elements of a new culture.

Thus, in 1907, a craft association was founded, the aim and object of which was set forth as "to ennoble industrial labor through the co-operation of art, industry and handicraft—by means of education, propaganda and united action on relevant questions." Admittance to the union was not by competition or recommendation. Membership was restricted to those invited to join by the executive committee. Thus, the union represented a selection of the very best of artistic talent, skill in craftsmanship and business idealism, and became an assembly of all the forces devoted to the ideal of quality in work. By a long series of exhibitions, by illustrated publications and finally by its magazine *Form,* devoted to all the varied problems of modern design, the union has performed a powerful educational work, among both producers and consumers. Inspired by the *Werkbund* idea, one of the leading companies for electrical appliances in Germany appointed no less a person than Peter Behrens as an artistic adviser to their works, not only to design their new factories but also to develop the forms of their products down to the smallest switch, and to supervise all their printed matter, from advertisements to letter heads.

The union has no exact parallel in other countries. A similar association was founded in England, but broke up after a short life without having gained any influence. Indeed, the *Werkbund* is a creation exactly characteristic of German idealism: an institution not involved in any kind of business interests, serving solely a cultural and ethical idea, namely to raise the morale of work. By this independent attitude soon acquiring a pubic reputation, the organization was able, through its influence, to affect public opinion, and, used and consulted by the Government on many occasions, it finally came to act as the organ of cultural consciousness of the nation.

NORTHERN VERSUS MEDITERRANEAN SPIRIT

It has already been mentioned that the new spirit of building first spread in northern Europe, with the Germanic countries well in the lead. We came upon its earliest manifestations in England; we then met it in Holland and Belgium. Here it re-

THEATRE, Cologne, 1914. Designed for the German
Werkbund Exhibition. Henry van de Velde, architect

TURBO FACTORY, Berlin, 1909. Peter Behrens, architect

STORE FOR F. L. AMES, Boston, 1886-1887. H. H. Richardson, architect

(Courtesy Department of Architecture, Museum of Modern Art, New York)

MARSHALL FIELD WHOLESALE BUILDING, Chicago, 1885-1887. H. H. Richardson, architect

(Courtesy Chicago Architectural Photographing Company)

ceived its strongest impulse with Henry van de Velde, the Fleming, who left his native country to make Germany the land of his adoption, where he found himself on the mother-ground of his proper Germanic-Nordic spirit. And in Germany, and her linguistically related neighbors, such as Holland, Austria and Switzerland, the new spirit of building achieved its strongest position. And this is not by chance. Because in the ideas of that new spirit, there unfolds anew that sort of creative instinct which is called intuitive imagination, an imagination particularly characteristic of Nordic, and especially perhaps of German architecture, which finds its greatest satisfaction in producing forms of individual character, developing the building out of the particular conditions, in contrast to the generalizing tendencies of Mediterranean classicism.

In fact, with the rise of the new spirit of building, this lasting contrast between Northern and Southern creative instincts developed into an actual combat. It is the eternal antithesis between intuitive and logical imagination, and their opposing principles of organic and mechanical order, which in this conflict enters a new and world-wide struggle for predominance.

This conflict, however, takes place within the larger sphere of that crisis of thought which in our time runs through the political, social and cultural life. It is but a partial aspect of that world-wide revolutionary movement, kindled and kept in motion by the growing resistance against obsolete forms of thought and habits of life that no longer correspond to the physical and spiritual necessities of actual life. The nature of this movement is revealed as a sincere effort of Man, as ardent as respectable, to overcome the present crisis of order by restoring the idea of organic order: a process of historic evolution which will not end until modern man has established a new cosmology, a new view of the world and of life.

3. THE ROLE OF AMERICA

The active part America played in the evolution of the new spirit of building was, of course, not confined to such bare utilitarian structures as silos and grain elevators, the simple geometric forms of which so deeply impressed the German architects of the *Art Nouveau* generation. In the domain of architecture, there are striking evidences in this country of an honest will to reform and of early efforts at re-thinking the basic problems of building, far ahead of the *Art Nouveau* movement, and also in part independent of the Arts-and-Crafts movement in England and the worthy example of William Morris. But the various attacks on the problem, undertaken by single courageous pioneers, remained isolated. They did not, as in Europe, kindle a general spiritual movement, springing from social rather than esthetic ideas and deeply grounded in the new social and industrial development; there was not, in America, a movement continued from generation to generation, spreading throughout the country, arousing public opinion, and finally shaking even the professionals from their academic conceptions. These American pioneers did not even induce the rise of a new school that would continue in the development of the new ideas. Is it due to the proverbial American individualism that the single efforts of clear-headed pioneers have not been consolidated in a new professional tradition?

However that may be, dealing with the rôle of America, we have to talk of individual achievements of single personalities rather than of general ideas realized by individuals and changing with their driving forces the spirit of building. In so doing, we select, in accordance with the method of this book, those personalities whose works not only reveal a new spirit, but are related to each other by a definite coherence and a certain sequence in their development. I refer, of course, to that radiant triple star represented by Henry Hobson Richardson, Louis Sullivan, and Frank Lloyd Wright.

RICHARDSON: FOUNDER OF A NEW AMERICAN VERNACULAR

H. H. Richardson was one of the first American architects who went to Paris to get his professional training at the Ecole des Beaux Arts. The formal discipline of that school provided him with the advantageous *routine d'atelier* exhibited throughout his work in the art of design and the skillful handling of the detail, such as color, ornament and decoration. Yet his strong character is proved by the fact that this formal education did not impair his realistic sense. Counterbalancing the one-sided training of the school by practical work, done in the ateliers of some Parisian architects, he kept an open and ingenious mind and never submerged himself in merely esthetic passions. By nature and talent a born architect, he succeeded in developing himself into a real builder rather than a draftsman and designer. At a time when architecture was debased by the activities of unscrupulous jerry-builders to a mere branch of commerce, these qualities were sufficient to make him a regenerator of building and the founder of a new American vernacular.

Living in a period of complete stylistic confusion, and still a period unable to think of its architectural problems in other than historical terms, what else could a young fervent architect do in order to find an inspiration but turn his attention to a primary style? Indeed, it proves the soundness of Richardson's instinct that he made the Romanesque style his choice. When, in the midst of a despairing decay in building, he was looking for a new discipline able to restore the dignity and integrity of architecture, this great style, imposing in its monumental grouping of masses and the expressive masonry of its strong walls, must have most nearly responded to his idea of real building: elemental, stable, and expressive of power.

But by selecting the Romanesque as the chief source of his inspiration he also revealed the narrow limits of his intention. His efforts were devoted to regaining solidity and esthetic quality in building. He was interested in the problems of monumental composition and the visual effects of vigorous masonry rather than in the structural problems arising with the technical innovations made in his time. Had he been interested in these actual problems of structure, he would, like Viollet-le-Duc, for instance, have followed the Gothic tradition. But, while the engineers of his time were working to develop new methods of construction, loosening and lightening the structure, he clung to somewhat reactionary methods of building, preferring heavy and rugged masonry, built of large-sized rough-hewn stone.

Nevertheless, using these materials and methods in a straightforward manner, with a fine feeling for their expressive qualities, he finally succeeded in developing a personal style, and gave his buildings a monumental character not seen in this country before. Outstanding examples of this famous Richardsonian manner are such well-known buildings as Trinity Church in Boston and the Pittsburgh Jail and Courthouse.

ON THE IDEA OF A PERSONAL STYLE IN ARCHITECTURE

But the typical monuments of the Richardsonian manner, a manner highly admired by contemporaries but soon thinned out by imitators, have mainly faded from interest, even if they have not been demolished in fact. Expressive as they are in their robust masonry and in the effective grouping of their large masses, piled up, as it seems, by the hands of a giant, they have proved to be the most transitory of his works. For this inner weakness with which they are afflicted, in spite of the freshness and vigor of their outer appearance, there is only one explanation. Being creations of a personal style, a virtue which roused the enthusiasm of the contemporaries, they are revealed to us as the limited offspring of the nineteenth century. This era with its general tendency towards individualism also furthered the idea of personal expression in architecture. Such an idea may be permitted to a genius like Michelangelo, although even this titan of architecture came to feel the danger of his individualistic experiments—look, for instance, at the Biblioteca Laurenziana, an example cited for that reason by Jakob Burckhardt "as instructive for ever, to the end of time." During the nineteenth century, this dangerous doctrine certainly tumbled architecture into the torrential whirls of subjectivism, and with the belief in the value of this idea, even the best and most brilliant architects came to grief: Richardson as well as Poelzig at a later period, and even van de Velde, the greatest theorist of the movement, who finally tried, in spite of his right and plain and straightforward theory, to realize his idea of a new style in a merely individual manner, in the way of personal expression.

In modern times, it has become, and still is at the present day, the tragedy of many talented architects, and especially of the strong and imaginative ones, that they believe in the sovereign consciousness of their own artistic personalities, that they can rise above the social conditions of their epoch; and so they exhaust their strength on ideas in which the age no longer believes, and which, in spite of all their abilities, they cannot actualize. Their works may be interesting, even admirable as documents of personal expression; yet they are not capable of further development, because they contain too much of personal caprice and special opportunity and contribute too little to the general problems of their time. In fact, the significance of any man of talent for his time, is precisely decided as he decides for himself in his work, in the choice of his problem and his attitude to it. And in the nineteenth century, that era of general transformation, the choices most urgently required of the architect concerned the new social and technical problems brought about by the far-reaching economic changes, and not the individual problem of a personal style. To attack these general problems, there was needed, however, a willingness to limit the freedom of the artistic personality in devotion to a super-personal necessity. And the solution of these new and urgent problems was retarded and postponed over and over again by the fact that so many architects of the nineteenth century were entirely absorbed by their individual problems, and put the satisfaction of their ego above collective needs.

CHARACTER OF THE NEW VERNACULAR

It is for that reason that the historical significance assigned to Richardson for developing a new spirit in building, has to be dated not so much from his large monumental buildings, which once established his name and fame, as from a series of smaller commissions he did in his mature years. In these buildings, although they are touched with historical reminiscences, he made the closest contact with his time. Look, for instance, at his small public libraries, particularly those in Quincy and North Easton. Here he achieved a new freedom of composition tending towards the functional arrangement of the plans, which in the exteriors finds its logical and effective expression in the free grouping of the parts and in the varying size of the windows and their disposition. And in the great series of railroad stations built for the Boston and Albany, he manifests a realistic conception which made these buildings not only structurally appropriate to their function, but also in form a true and clear expression of their purpose. With their simple elements, their low walls and broadly expanded masses, with their sloping roofs and projecting sheds running along the tracks, they reveal a character immediately felt as modern.

BOSTON AND ALBANY STATION, Auburndale, Mass., 1881.
H. H. Richardson, architect
(Courtesy Department of Architecture, Museum of Modern Art, New York)

R. T. PAINE HOUSE, Waltham, Mass., 1884-1886.
H. H. Richardson, architect
(Courtesy Department of Architecture, Museum of Modern Art, New York)

WAINWRIGHT BUILDING, St. Louis, 1890-1891. Louis Sullivan, architect

(Courtesy Keystone-Underwood)

SCHLESINGER-MEYER BUILDING, Chicago, 1899-1904. Louis Sullivan, architect

(Courtesy Chicago Architectural Photographing Company)

The same is true for some of his later works in the field of domestic architecture. Besides the virtues of their plans, well thought out in the arrangement of the rooms and their inner relation according to their function, these houses show a new device in their exteriors. They manifest a change of mind—from monumentalizing the building into humanizing it. And as to the materials, it is obvious that their use has been more naturalized. The Richardsonian preference for rough masonry still remains, but its Cyclopean forms have been modified to a scale appropriate to civil manners. And then, and even better, there is the rediscovery of wood, which since Colonial times has been the native building material in the United States, and which now appears again in the shingle walls and roofs of many of these houses. As a matter of fact, Richardson's public buildings, with their intentional, and therefore somewhat artificial, monumentality, might have been built anywhere, in Europe as well as America—and his design for the Albany Cathedral anticipated, indeed, as Lewis Mumford observed in "The Brown Decades," Schwechten's Kaiser Wilhelm Gedächtnis-Kirche in Berlin. But such houses as the Paine House in Waltham, Massachusetts, the Potter House in St. Louis and the Ames Gate Lodge and Gardener's Cottage in North Easton, Massachusetts, reveal a typical American face, with characteristic features stamped by the natural environment in which they were built. They are grown on American ground and breathe the air of the land. It is for these buildings that Richardson has to be called the founder of a new American vernacular, as capable as it is worthy of further development.

NEW BUILDING HEIGHTS

During the eighties, the rapid growth of cities caused by the new industrial development brought about an equally rapid increase of land values and opened new ground for exploitation. Not checked by restrictive building laws or creative methods of city planning, which would insure the wise use of land, speculative enterprise pleaded for greater building heights. In 1884, William LeBaron Jenney erected for the Home Insurance Company in Chicago an office building of ten stories, using a new construction of iron frame work which he deliberately sheathed with masonry walls. When, in the following year, Richardson was commissioned to build the Marshall Field Store in Chicago, planned for seven stories only, he insisted upon the use of sturdy masonry, relying on a traditional construction proved as certain, rather than on a technical innovation not yet tried as to its solidity. He erected a large square block reduced to the simplest form with almost no architectural detail. But above the broad basis of the building the massive walls are opened up by wide windows, admitting large amounts of light into the interior. In the façades, several stories are grouped together under a series of lofty arches providing the broad-spread mass of the building with a definite verticalism.

This tendency towards lightening the building bulk was continued and pushed to a climax in the Pray Building in Boston, erected in 1886, the year Richardson died at the age of forty-eight, ending a most promising career before it had developed into full maturity. With this building Richardson surpassed himself: it is perhaps the best and certainly the most important of his works. The outer walls, built in brick, are reduced to small sturdy piers, rising up to the height of five stories and connected by wide arches which support the attic and the heavy corbeled cornice. The spandrels are reduced to the thickness of the interior floors. Thus the design, already bearing in its main lines the characteristic features of the steel frame construction, offered an inspiring example for the solution of the structural problem now arising with the general use of this new method of building.

LOUIS SULLIVAN: THE FOUNDER OF A NEW THEORY

This very problem of structure was first systematically attacked in this country by Louis Henry Sullivan, born in Boston in 1856. He was not only a great artist, a splendid draftsman endowed with all the esthetic faculties that make up a great architect; his was also an original mind, a fresh and independent nature that soon found itself in strong disagreement with the surrounding world. And suffering from the conditions he had to live in, he turned to thinking, as passionately as impatiently, seeking an answer to the perplexing problems that crowded upon him from all sides.

Sullivan attended the Massachusetts Institute of Technology, where he had to learn the five classic orders of architecture. But the lifeless method of academic training, based on the doctrine that architectural perfection can only be achieved by using the vocabulary of the historical styles, evoked in him the definite conviction that architecture was a dead art. He then went to Paris and spent two years at the Ecole des Beaux Arts, considered as "the fountainhead of theory," and was dissatisfied, too. The discipline of this school, as he points out in his autobiography, "settled down to a theory of plan, yielding results of extraordinary brilliancy, but which, after all, was not the reality he sought." To him it was "but an abstraction, a method that was intellectual and esthetic, a state of mind that was local and specific, not universal." This statement should be taken to heart as a warning of the danger involved in any kind of merely academic education.

There were, however, two events in his formative years, when he set out to find this "universal," which deeply impressed his mind and definitely directed his mode of thinking. In Paris, when preparing his entrance examinations for the Beaux Arts, he took lessons with M. Clopet, a tutor in Mathematics. At their first meeting, the pupil brought an American text book on Descriptive Geometry; but the teacher, looking the book over, discovered that to each theorem there was "a procession of exceptions and special cases." He suggested throwing the book in the waste basket. "We shall not have need of it here; for here our demonstrations shall be so broad as to admit of no exception." As these startling words flashed through his mind, there arose, to use his own words, a vision and a fixed resolve: "If it can be done in Mathematics, why not in Architecture? It shall be! No one has—I will!"

The other event took place in Chicago, where fate threw in his path young John Edelmann, of German descent, philosophically minded and a keen thinker like Sullivan himself. He was foreman in the office of William LeBaron Jenney, where Sullivan found his first job. Once in the course of their endless youthful discussions he flung out to Sullivan the startling phrase, "suppressed functions"—inspiring words which opened up to him another vision. There is no one who has not some time in his life experienced the enlightening force of a plain single word that strikes him in reading or conversation; and he knows how such a word, at the right moment, may light up the inner and outer world, opening a new path to consciousness. This happened to Sullivan: it was the *Zeitgeist,* indeed, which through Edelmann spoke to him at this historical moment, and its magic words laid the foundations of his thoughts and determined the goal of his life: to make architecture again a living art of contemporary immediate value.

When the word "function" was detonated by the word "suppressed," a new synthesis articulated itself within him. If architecture was to revive, it must intelligently serve—it must not suppress. With this elemental perception, he set out to develop a new philosophy of architecture, based on a principle of general validity, putting to test a rule "so broad as to admit of no exceptions." Expressing no more than a simple biological truth, stating the morphological law of all organic growth, he finally formulated this guiding principle in the words: "Form follows function."

In this simple formula, the new spirit of building acquired its *credo.*

"BEAUTY THE PROMISE OF FUNCTION"

The essence of this functionalist theory was in the air all through the nineteenth century, in this country as well as in Europe. It might well be that Sullivan breathed it in as a boy, when he lived in Boston. Here it was that Horatio Greenough, the sculptor, as early as the forties had set forth in his lectures and writings a principle of structure revealed to him in nature: "the primal law of unflinching adaptation of form to function." This structural law, he found, obtained in the forms of the clipper-ship and the "American trotting-wagon," and he referred his readers to these examples as demonstrating "an organization in which every advance in performance has been an advance in expression, in grace, in grandeur, in beauty, according to the functions of the craft." Architecture, instead of forcing the functions of every sort of building into one general formula, should learn from these models the principle of adapting the structure to the stern organic requirements of the needs.

In one of his essays, published in H. T. Tuckerman's *Memorial of Horatio Greenough,* he precisely defined Beauty as the promise of Function; Action as the presence of Function; Character as the record of Function. And maintaining that the first downward step in art was the introduction of the first unorganic, non-functional element, whether of shape or color, he condemned the false conception of a merely sensuous beauty, of an "arbitrary embellishment, not yet organically explained or determined."

Van Wyck Brooks, in *The Flowering of New England,* refers

116

to a letter Greenough wrote to Emerson, in which he sums up his theory of structure: "A scientific arrangement of spaces and forms to functions and to site; an emphasis of features proportioned to their *gradated* importance in function; color and ornament to be decided and arranged and varied by strictly organic laws, having a distinct reason for each decision; the entire and immediate banishment of all makeshift and make-believe."

No doubt Greenough, like many another advanced thinker of his age, had in his hands all the essential elements of a new theory of structure. However, it was left to the following generation to tie these elements together, and it was Louis Sullivan who according to Hugh Morrison, his biographer, first succeeded in setting forth both by precept and by example a new theory of organic building.

THE RISE OF THE SKYSCRAPER

Sullivan undertook a long series of practical experiments in developing an architecture that fitted its functions, "a new realistic architecture," to use his own words, based on well-defined needs and practical conditions, which no architectural dictum, or tradition, or superstition, or habit should stand in the way of. The eighties, full of robust realism in technique, science and economics, were well prepared for such a decisive attempt at a realistic architecture. With the advance of urbanization a great many new building types had come into being, throwing up a host of new architectural problems which urgently called for a practical solution. Among these new types the tall office building, rapidly multiplying its stories and extending skywards, was certainly the most conspicuous one. And it is with this type that Sullivan found his first chance to put his theory to a practical test. At the age of thirty, he designed, as partner of Dankmar Adler, the Auditorium Building in Chicago: a ten-story building only, but sheltering in its huge body such heterogeneous utilities as offices, a hotel with its various accessories, and finally a large theater with about three thousand seats.

In his project, Sullivan included the main parts of the building in a large block of square form, crowned by an effective tower: a genuine piece of architecture with well-marked contour, plain surface and clear articulation. As for the outer aspect of the building he consciously joined the thread that Richardson had begun to spin in the Marshall Field Store, applying to the structure a decided verticalism, grouping several stories into a unit and lightening the heavy masses of masonry.

The next year he built the Wainwright Building in St. Louis. Applying in this project the new steel skeleton construction, he soon recognized that the change in the structural system meant a radical revolution in architecture, overthrowing the traditional idea of building mass related to supporting walls. In the skeleton construction, the outer walls are no longer weight-bearing, but are themselves supported by the horizontal beams: a kind of sheathing or shell, covering the steel frame-work. Trying to express this changed function of the walls, Sullivan dissolved in his project the outer walls into a long row of narrow piers carried through in strong verticality from the base to the widely projecting cornice, which gives with its heavy shadows a well-marked termination to the building. With this articulated verticalism accentuating the lightness and loftiness of the building, the architect accomplished a double purpose: he served the practical needs of the office building by providing with this system of fenestration a great quantity of light and air, and he also developed an emotional effect by the rapidly soaring lines of his vigorous tower. But he certainly missed the solution to the architectural problem involved in this new type of structure; and it has to be admitted that Richardson in his design for the Pray Building in Boston, though carried out in masonry, came closer to the solution than Sullivan when he built the Wainwright Building in skeleton construction. The accentuated verticalism applied for its design is not logically derived from the steel cage system which is rather a structure of square frames, but from the urge to emotional expression which proved once more to be stronger than his faith in the principle that form follows function.

As a practical demonstration of the theory, the Monadnock block, built in Chicago by Burnham and Root in 1891, was far more advanced, although in its sixteen stories masonry was still employed. Following its function as an office building it was designed as a simple box, built in brick, the plain walls pierced with openings, in their size reduced to two recurring standards. To this stern façade a strong rhythm is given by a series of projecting bay windows, a form in this case chosen not for merely decorative, but for functional purposes, as supplying with its curved surface an increase of light for the rooms. The architectural effect of the building, made of its own elements only and avoiding all ornamental detail, rests upon the discipline of its

order and proportions. In a surrounding of commercial buildings, all lavish with palatial luxury, it needed an intrepid and
uncompromising spirit to erect a building of such a rugged, almost repelling character. In its rigid functionalism, demonstrating a new conception, it became a landmark of modern building: the architect, as an artistic personality, steps back behind
the commission given to him by society. In an act of self-denial,
he puts his individual forces into service for common needs, arising from the new social evolution.

In this attitude is manifested the truth that building is a social
art. The consequence of this conception, which has become the
guiding idea of the new spirit of building, is the general effort
to bring building again into a reasonable organic relation to the
actual social and economic world, thereby re-establishing that
indispensable identity between the content and the form of life,
which is missed in the works of those who have turned their
backs on their time.

Now, as to the skyscraper, Sullivan, as a far-sighted and social-
minded spirit, denied the justification of this new type of building, realizing that it was a mere offspring of speculative business
and its undisciplined forces. As an architect, however, attracted
by its architectural problem appealing so strongly to imagination, he took an immense interest and a practical part in its development. In his own conception of the problem, he came to
the closest realization of his theory, when he built the Schle-
singer and Mayer Building (now that of Carson, Pirie Scott Co.)
in Chicago. With this building, erected about 1900, he practically demonstrated his conviction that "every problem has its

solution within itself." In the design, any remembrance of the traditional idea of masonry has disappeared. Its main features clearly manifest the skeleton system used for the construction: the architectural lines follow exactly the form of the steel frame, the windows are enlarged to the full width of the frames, and the large openings are only separated by small vertical piers. With its emphasized horizontalism derived from the continuous bands of spandrels between long rows of broad windows, the design anticipated a pattern that soon became characteristic for the works of modern architecture. And while the upper part of the building, almost bare of architectural detail, presents for the first time a strict and logical solution of the problem in question, the urge and pleasure of self-expression, never put fully at rest in an artist, is worked off on the two lower stories, the only ones which are really visible at a glance from the street. Their walls are covered with a rich ornament of the most fanciful design, executed in a fine, lacy grille-work.

Demonstrating the brilliancy of Sullivan's draftsmanship and the originality and abundance of his fantasy, this ornament is certainly the most personal, but also the most transient part of his work. Though it is exclusively based on naturalistic motives, in the conduct of its sweeping and swinging lines, its design bears an obvious similarity to the abstract ornament of the *Art Nouveau* movement, therewith proving a striking continuity of the time in the forms of artistic expression. Within Sullivan's work, this ornament, springing from the unappeased desire for personal expression in architecture, remains a residue of the nineteenth century.

But while Sullivan, the architect, with one foot was still standing on the individualistic ideas of the past, with the other foot he already stood on the ground of the twentieth century. And as a philosopher, he certainly looked far ahead of his time, helping with his theoretical contributions the new spirit of building to become conscious. And he knew how to formulate the results of his thinking in excellent writings. His two books, *Kindergarten Chats* and *The Autobiography of an Idea,* are rich sources of ideas on the nature of building. He plainly points out in these books that building is a social manifestation, and if we want better building, we must first have a better society. As an architect, the author had learned by experience that to restore architecture to a living art is beyond the power of a single individual, even if he be a genius in the art. He knew that this task needed for its solution a collective effort, and that this effort could only be successful if it were sincerely supported by society. "What the people are within, the buildings express without; and inversely, what the buildings are objectively is a sure index of what the people are subjectively." But it was the voice of the preacher in the desert. His teachings did not turn the American mind. His fermenting ideas were neither echoed by a revolutionary movement, nor followed by a new school. Even his practical work, revealing so many spores of a new creative efflorescence, depended for its continuation upon two eyes, which were Frank Lloyd Wright's, his only important disciple.

ACADEMIC REACTION

The tragic fate of the United States, its inability to achieve spiritual continuity, to build up an artistic tradition of its own, soon became once more obvious. The promising seed that Sullivan had sowed in American ground with his bold experiments towards a realistic architecture based upon the principle of organic order, was buried before germination had taken place under the White City of gypsum which formed the architecture of the Chicago World's Exposition in 1893.

The great world's fair is a typical modern institution that arose with the nineteenth century, and hitherto it had been used for demonstrative experiments in progressive building; the Great International Exposition in London, in 1851, for instance, set the first landmark in modern building with Paxton's Crystal Palace, and for the Exposition at Paris in 1889, Gustave Eiffel built his great tower, demonstrating the potentialities of the new iron construction. At Chicago, however, this extraordinary chance was deliberately excluded from the beginning. At the decisive meeting of the commission of artists in whose hands the planning work was laid, it was resolved to use for the Exposition "the classic motive." The feelings, the mind and the mode of thinking from which such a decision was derived, were best characterized, when during this meeting one of the members of the commission, overwhelmed with the greatness of the moment, burst out in the ecstatic words: "Do you realize that this is the greatest meeting of artists since the fifteenth century!" In this historical meeting, difficult though it is to believe, the vigorous

Spirit of Chicago, always famous for its industrial energy and practical capacity, and just revealing its vitality anew in its progressive commercial building, was subjected to the reactionary spirit of a small group of Eastern architects, who pleaded for making the Exposition a stupendous demonstration of good taste, to which they themselves made the most distinct pretensions. Thus, instead of challenging the new spirit of building to manifest what building would be in the future, the Exposition was to be a spectacular show of academic design, as intentionally as immodestly rivaling the classic monuments of the past.

The Chicago Exposition has been called a turning point in American taste; and, in fact, it helped to inaugurate in town planning the idea of the "City Beautiful" and in architecture an academic reaction which dominated the next generation. The relapse into what is called "good taste" also interrupted, in this country, the formative process of the new spirit of building for many years to come. A year after the Chicago Fair, the American Academy of Art was established at Rome, where young architects, who in former days had gone to the Beaux Arts in Paris, from now on went to get their training in good taste. Good taste, however, is never a definitive quality of the genuine artist; in the domain of art it is rather a substitute for creative impulse.

The best characterization of the Chicago Exposition, disclosing what it was supposed to be and what, instead, it finally became, was formulated by Charles Eliot Norton in one of his lectures on "Art in America." And as this respected American who gave at Harvard the first University instruction in the history

124

of fine arts as related to social progress and general culture, also refers in his criticism to the influence of social conditions on the standard of building, it is appropriate to quote a few paragraphs.

"Not one of those great façades was an expression of the plan, construction or purpose of the building behind it. The buildings were simply masked by full-sized models of decorative walls. They were intended for scenic effect; they were magnificent decorative pieces. . . . They expressed the wealth, the ingenuity, the practical capacity of the people; but they were not the creations in which the vital spirit of a nation expressed itself by means of noble organic structures vitalized by its own superabundant life. . . .

"Here was the United States on show, both in real aspects and in its potentialities. It was an exhilarating spectacle . . . full of material promise. Was it full also of spiritual promise? . . . This question will be answered only as the course of years rolls on. If the heterogeneous millions of American people rise slowly to the height of their unexampled opportunities; if gradually they become unified in sentiment, with common ideals of noble national existence; if mastering the materializing influences of their present conditions, they assimilate the elements of material prosperity so as to make them contribute to spiritual growth; if they turn the products of the understanding into nutriment for the reason and the imagination—then we may be sure that the life of the nation will find natural expression in an art which shall be a fresh revelation of the highest powers of the human spirit, and in which the beauty of those new ideals which lie as yet vague and shapeless in the heart of our democracy shall be embodied in forms of enduring delight and inspiration."

In the White City of the Chicago Exposition, there was only one monument of progress: the Transportation Building, designed by Louis Sullivan. Except in some unessential details, this building was already free from historical style forms, and it showed in its noble simplicity and severe monumentality the guiding line which ought to have been followed throughout the entire work. It stood alone in this debauch of good taste, as its architect in his later life stood alone, an embittered man, abandoned by his friends, discouraged by the adverse course of events, and in spite of his enormous gifts rarely commissioned, and then only for insignificant jobs. Most of his late designs were for small bank buildings, erected in little provincial towns in the Middle West. And these buildings show in their general attitude, in their forms and proportions, in the use of material and treatment of detail, a remarkable new note; a note which shows, a fact as rare as strange, the reacting influence of the disciple on the master.

FRANK LLOYD WRIGHT: FOUNDER OF AN ORGANIC ARCHITECTURE

Before Frank Lloyd Wright became Sullivan's pupil, he received the beginnings of professional training at the University of Wisconsin, where he attended an engineering course. Perhaps it is due to this realistic rather than formal education that, when he later became an architect, he was never benumbed by the academic dogma. From the start he preferred to be animated by the individual conditions of the problem at hand rather than to be confined to the general rules of the geometric law. To start from necessity, to proceed on the demands of service and efficiency, and not from random abstractions which escape from life: that was to the man sympathetic to the engineer an obligation as strong as self-evident.

With Wright's work the principle of organic structure recurred on a higher level. With him architecture, after having grown torpid through excessive occupation with the masterpieces of the past, turned decidedly to the rejuvenating sources of its strength: to Nature. But this new turn towards nature manifests itself not in an intentional naturalism, but in a new mode of thinking about the structure. In one of his earliest manifestoes, Wright declared: "Although for centuries our practice has been to turn from nature, seeking inspiration in books, adhering slavishly to dead formulas, her wealth of suggestion is inexhaustible, her riches greater than any man's desire. . . ." And he continues: "A sense of the organic in Nature is indispensable to an architect, and the knowledge of the relation of form to function is at the root of his practice."

These few sentences characterize clearly and comprehensively the spiritual standpoint, which shows, even in the formulation, a striking congruity with the principal belief of Goethe expressed in one of his Essays on Art, when he said: "An universal knowledge of organic nature is necessary in order to understand and develop the artist through the labyrinth of his structure." Wright's reflection of nature is, conforming to the classic example of Goethe, of that creative kind, where "intuition itself becomes thinking, and thinking an intuition." It is directed upon the morphological, upon the problem of structure, and upon the laws of organic growth. From the study of nature and its formative laws, he gets a firm and definite conception for his architectural creation. He realizes "how form derives its structure from nature and from the character of the material and its conditions, exactly as a flower forms itself according to the law which lies in its seed." Subjecting the structure of building, with the severest logic, to the laws upon which all organic growth rests, he succeeded in reaching beyond the results that realistic architecture had hitherto achieved, deliberately based as it was on a one-sided rationalistic concept, and pushed on to forms of higher organic order. It was he who first brought the idea of organic structure defined in the striking formula of his master-teacher to realization: a new architectural form. And the sensuous effect of this form has evidently not suffered because the creative instinct was guided by a cognition derived from natural science. The result is not only convincing by its logic; it also gives delight through the manifold imaginativeness of the form. This form, stimulating by its fullness of nature and nearness to life, immediately appeals to intuition and feeling, enchanting the senses with the melody of its language and the expressive grace of its appearance.

A DEMONSTRATION OF ORGANIC PLANNING

One must consider the plans of Wright's buildings in detail in order to understand the change in the principle of structure and the working of the new law. The ground-plan shows itself freed from the rigid doctrine of geometric order. Mathematics, as is proper in the realm of art, has sunk from the commanding position as a determinant of the law of the form and structure to that of an auxiliary rôle: it has become a technical subsidiary science. With this new spirit in building, space has lost its architectural sovereignty. For it is not the aim in forming the structure to represent the geometric idea of space, but to create for the individual life, which unfolds itself within that space, an accurately adjusted shell. This explains the strange irregularity of these plans, which exhibit irregular contours with numerous projections, and also single rooms of various shapes with manifold juttings and recessions.

And with the conception of space the manner of arranging the rooms also changes. The plan is no longer a geometric distribution of rooms attached by principle to a system of axes, but the rooms are arranged so that they complement each other in their services, forming in their totality a uniformly functioning whole. And in their connection, the rooms are so bound to one another, spliced like muscles, that by their inner tension they are brought into indissoluble cohesion. At first, this new method of joining the rooms was accomplished by arranging, as connecting links, short lobby-like passages between the main rooms, effecting an almost imperceptible flowing of the rooms into one another. Later, this method was felt to be too loose, and replaced by an interlacing of rooms, at times increased toward bold penetrations, so that it seems as though one room were evolving out of another. And the more the inner structure strengthened, the looser became its outer contour. The more the sureness in the mastery of the new laws increased, the freer and opener became the contours of the ground-plan. In the projects in which Wright has achieved the maturity of his style, the rooms are arranged around the nucleus of the chimney part, like leaves of a plant around their stem. Radiating as if from a power center, they reach out into the garden and the landscape, opening themselves to the light and the view on all sides.

TOWARDS AN ORGANIC FORM

In the same manner that the plan in all its parts forms an indissoluble whole, so, according to the law of organic growth, are the ground-plan and elevation inseparably united with one another. "An organic form," Wright has said, "grows its own structure out of conditions as a plant grows out of the soil: both unfold similarly from within." In this sense, the laws of organic planning find their continuation and completion in the external structure; and the manifold arrangement of the parts, the lively grouping of building masses, are to be viewed as the result of the inner logic of design, and not as a brilliant show-piece of a deliberately picturesque composition. As to these buildings, one had better avoid speaking of "composition" at all, since no less a man than Goethe has condemned this expression, in nature as well as in art, as degrading. "The organs do not compose themselves as if already previously finished," he said; "they develop themselves together and out of one another, to an existence which necessarily takes part in the whole." Wright's buildings are neither designed nor composed; they are built and created in three dimensions as coherent organisms. It is for that reason that his buildings have no definite main view or any real façade at all. As a plant viewed from any angle appears in its

ISABEL ROBERTS HOUSE, River Forest, Ill., 1907. Frank Lloyd Wright, architect *(Courtesy Department of Architecture, Museum of Modern Art, New York)*

COONLEY HOUSE, Riverside, Ill., 1908. Frank Lloyd Wright, architect *(Courtesy Department of Architecture, Museum of Modern Art, New York)*

TALIESIN II, Spring Green, Wis., 1914-1915

TALIESIN III (Built after Taliesin II was razed by fire), 1925. Frank Lloyd Wright, architect *(Courtesy Department of Architecture, Museum of Modern Art, New York)*

full beauty and always offers new charms, so the nature of these buildings can only be experienced by encircling them. Whatever the perspective may be to the building, it always offers new aspects, full of variety, and only in the succession of one upon the other is there disclosed the nature and meaning of the whole.

Speaking of the structure of these buildings, it is not by chance that one is, again and again, urged to a comparison with the world of plants. Like a plant, the building grows up from the earth to the light. Above a compact base unfolds a loosened bulk, developed into rich plastic form through the harmonic interplay of its necessary parts and through the extended fullness of its appropriate detail. And in the development of this detail any trace of a leaning upon historic examples has been eradicated. It is in its form entirely independent, and new, also, in the sense of being organic. "Form," Wright once said, "is made by function, but qualified by use. Therefore, form changes with changing conditions." It is the aim of this new art of detail to develop every form to complete individuality, according to the individual conditions from which it grows and which, therefore, are studied with an incomparable degree of sensibility.

Here it becomes clear how the creative observation of nature turns into a new artistic vision. Take, for instance, the horizontal slabs boldly projected, that new motive which has been the most imitated in modern building: in these widely overhanging eaves, spreading themselves canopy-like over terraces and balconies, there seems to be plantlike existence translated into architectural form. Or again, look at the changing forms of the windows, their distribution, their arrangement in groups of rhythmic order, in which the law seems to repeat itself that determines the ranging and ranking of leaves. Notice the delicate relation between the building bulk and the detail: as the bulk rises higher from the ground it becomes looser and lighter, while the detail becomes more elaborate and more tenuous. Notice finally the new development of the roofs, which free themselves from the substructure through widely overhanging projections, and spread like lofty tree-tops, making the house with its loosened silhouette stand out against the horizon. There may creep in, at times, something too "motive-like"; there may occasionally be found in this new art of detail a relapse into compositional tendencies opposed to the command of artistic economy: the excess is easily attributable to the exuberant joy in the new vision, and considering the enrichment of form gained thereby, and its emotional effects, we will always feel our objections weakened.

It is quite within the sphere of this new vision that it also turns its special attention to the effects of light, and beyond this, also includes in the artistic calculation the air. Wright treats light as if it were a natural building material. The graduated interplay of light and shade is to him an artistic medium of expression. The broad shadows, cast by the widely projecting eaves and roofs, shade off the plastic modeling, and the changing contrasts of light and dark underline the dynamics of the building groups. And similarly, the air is evaluated as an element of form, is drawn into the concept of building. Wright splits the building mass up, he loosens its volume, since he intermingles it with open air-space. With this inclusion of the air-space in the formation, there is accomplished an intimate connection of the inside with the outside, a new feature which from now on becomes the unmistakable characteristic of the modern house. "Wright," said one of his German critics, "is the first architect to whom the atmosphere is more than mere background to his works. He uses it, he calculates with it, again and again he tries to relate his work so finely with the atmosphere that both must seem indissolubly connected. His entire system of projecting flat roofs, the inclusion of air-space within the building, and the concentration of shadow, in contrast to the rows of loosened, almost light-drinking windows in the upper stories, serves unconsciously this goal. Almost everywhere he tries, with the most varied means, to create between the outer world and the building intermediate bodies, forming transitions and sympathetically and more fully molding the relation between the two, taking all harshness from the fusion."

The new relation to nature and to organic life, from which the fundamental ideas of Wright's art are derived, is finally revealed in the changed treatment of the material. Wright uses, as a rule, the material in the sense of its organic nature. For him the material is by nature a willing friend, and everything depends upon hewing out of it, through careful treatment, its essential peculiarity. Veneration for nature forbids him to destroy the natural grain of the wood; he never uses covering paint, but leaves the wood in its simple state, shows the chance work of its branching, or treats it at times with colored stains. In the same manner he turns to account the structure of plaster and of bricks, the surface glazing of ceramic tiles, the nature of stone, its jointing and its size, utilizing not only the physical but also

the physiognomical properties of the material, in order to enhance the individualizing characteristics of his building. And
never is there a casual, or even conflicting juxtaposition of materials: they are harmoniously connected with each other and
organically joined in the sense of a natural common union.

"OUT OF THE EARTH, INTO THE SUN"

This live feeling for materials is another reason why Wright's
buildings fit so naturally in their surroundings. They are built
into nature, almost bred into the life-space of their surrounding landscape. The majority of the country houses he built are
on the wide plains of the Middle West, that solemn landscape
consisting of luxuriant vegetation with ancient timber-lands, of
gentle far-ranging hills and an endless horizon. The houses with
their broad masses widely spread out, with their low proportions
and the long horizontal lines of their roofs, follow these large
contours of the landscape. Like dense thickets, rooted firmly in
the earth, their low building-masses stretch out over the ground,
always turning towards the light, following the natural tendencies of the site, adapting themselves pliantly to every fold of
land, every elevation of ground, with far-stretched low walls
framing the garden, trees and other vegetation of the surroundings and pulling them, as if with fangs, inward to the house.

The domestic buildings of Wright are like Japanese houses,
so fitted into the landscape that the building almost impercep-
tibly blends with surrounding nature. The Japanese house manifests the same spirit of nature, the same tendency toward an
organic structure. It also shows this intimate connection with

the scene it is set in, this multiform arrangement of roofs meticulously calculated in its effects, and the careful treatment of materials according to their physical and physiognomical properties. It is not by chance that Wright's country houses recall the Japanese pattern. He was several times in Japan for long intervals (and in Tokio he even built a hotel which though one of his largest works is certainly not his best). The philosophy of a country where man merges in nature, and a civilization where art and life permeate each other so intimately, must have been especially favorable to his own conception of art. Wright's art is, in fact, similar to the Japanese, nature-like and rural; and it evidently loses its greatest values when it is diverted to projects of typical city building.

Wright's decided preference for low building corresponds to this pastoral character. He certainly knows the satisfaction of being able to build everything on the ground level, and he knows how to prize it, this "highest happiness of the architect": he has tasted it to the full in his own house Taliesin, which in its high perfection is to date his most mature work. In its organic structure and its intimate connection with nature, this house may justly take as its due the famous words of praise which Vasari coined for Raphael's Villa Farnesina: "non murato, ma veramente nato."

WRIGHT THE ARTIST

Each house of Wright's is an individual organism, related in every detail to man, alive in itself, friendly to all life, and in complete harmony with nature, a growth. Always starting from the stern command of use, Wright tries to develop the form of the structure out of its functions; he tries to articulate the individual nature of each building, and to unfold this nature in its own world, in its own proper life-space, according to its immanent law. From this conception derives the stupendous manifoldness of his form, and the incomparable art of imbuing with character every part which marks the summit of his mastery.

Wright's work reveals a new conception of the idea of organic structure. The creative observation of nature which led him to that conception, and the stating of the morphological problem involved in it, is alone an achievement of extraordinary intellectuality. No less important is the architectural achievement with which the new idea of structure gained its artistic presentation. In it there is revealed the unfathomable strength of his intuition and the abundance of creative power with which he is gifted. From these extraordinary faculties there originated the inexhaustible richness of his form. His work is full of form, like nature herself whose laws are at the basis of his work. In every detail this law is evident, and yet the command of its necessity is followed with complete inner freedom. In the work itself the principle on which it is based has been completely absorbed, so that it constitutes not a demonstration but a work of art unfolding a new form of beauty. The form always binds itself to its law, but it yet remains free from any dogmatic inhibitions. It has been worked out with the most exacting care and with full technical conscientiousness. It makes copious use of modern building materials, of glass, iron and cement; it tries to utilize the new constructive possibilities in a functional way and to interpret their character in new architectural forms. It also makes use of the machine as a willing tool. And while so doing, it loses nothing of its lyrical charm, nothing of the impetuous boldness which completes the varying perspectives in their daring but always organic asymmetries.

A marginal note may be added. Jakob Burckhardt, the justly famous historian of Renaissance architecture, used to say that one must have money as well as luck and humor for the pleasure, so questionable to him, of creating an unsymmetric building. This pious prescription has been fulfilled for Wright in so far as he has almost always been able to build for the more affluent, who have placed at his command large, and even unusual, means. Thanks to this economic independence his forms have often been developed to a degree of lavishness that may very well represent the prosperity of their patrons, but has been to their creator rather a misfortune than an advantage. The abundance of means entices him into artistic effects, and to the degree to which these effects are sought for their own sake the work is removed from the principles on which it is based. Wright disposes of an abundance of fancy which is powerful enough to be the stock of a dozen architects. And this blossoming and luxuriant imagination, the strongest of his manifold talents, is also a danger. It undermines his artistic discipline, and sometimes lures him with its precious gifts into being unfaithful to his own theory, so that, as J. J. P. Oud remarked to the point, "Wright the artist renounces what Wright the prophet proclaims."

Wright's ornament, the product of his exuberant fancy, is like Sullivan's the most accidental and the most transitory part of his work: it proves that even he was confined to the limits of his generation. But leaving aside these rankly growing accessories, considering first the structure of his domestic buildings, and then studying the programmatic statements of his numerous manifestoes, one gets, indeed, a clear and thoroughly definite idea of the structural principles of modern building, which meanwhile have become international common property.

SUMMARY

"The creation of an organic style," to quote Burckhardt once more, "depends upon high gifts and a great piece of good fortune, and particularly upon a definite degree of unbiassed naïvety and fresh nearness to nature." There are good reasons, he added, why the phenomenon has appeared only twice in the history of art.

All the conditions stated prove true for Frank Lloyd Wright. As an artist he really is nature, and a great contribution towards developing this nature and preserving its originality is certainly made by the great and unique landscape, in which he was brought up and which, as an elemental experience, impregnated his creative instinct. Developing a local American vernacular with his so-called "prairie-style," he also inaugurated, through the personal achievements of his singular talent, a new organic style which is now affirming itself throughout the world: a new style for whose acceptance the intellectual life of the times has long been ready, and for which the intellectual ground has been prepared.

In his own country, however, Wright's work has been scarcely

138

understood, and its influence has been very small. In his autobiography Wright tells of a visit once paid to his workshop by
Kuno Francke, the German professor of philosophy, at that time
exchange-professor in esthetics at Harvard. The visitor, after
having studied his work, wanted him to go to Germany to stay
and carry on his work. "I see you are doing 'organically,' " he
said, "what my people are feeling for only superficially. They
would reward you. It will be long before your own people will
be ready for what you are trying to give them." As a matter of
fact, Wright's fame was first established in Europe where his
work was immediately understood, and it was taken up with
enthusiasm in Germany, where a complete monograph was published as early as 1910, perhaps as the result of Kuno Francke's
short visit.

Without being guilty of exaggeration, one may justly assert
that Frank Lloyd Wright's work is the first creation in the realm
of architecture that can be regarded as an independent contribution of the American spirit to European culture. In Europe this
work happened to fall in with the progressive movement which
for a century had nurtured a new spirit in building, and Wright,
with his pure examples of organic structure, full of an unusual
and exhilarating beauty, gave this movement a fresh and strong
impulse.

PART THREE

THE ADVENT OF A NEW STYLE

1. FROM PERSONAL EXPRESSION
TOWARDS A NEW STYLE

REACTIONS TO THE WORLD WAR

Art is subjected to continuous change by the changes in civilization. The nineteenth century, that epoch of triumphant individualism, was in art a period of great personalities, coming to flower in as many styles as there were individuals capable of personal style. In architecture probably the last of these great personalities to assert himself was Frank Lloyd Wright. His art is founded on a principle of general validity, the principle of organic structure which must be the guiding principle of the future, if architecture is again to be a living art. Yet the form in which Wright realizes and represents this general principle is unique: a personal creation, worthy of highest esteem, as a product of an exuberant imagination, full of grace and serenity, of gaiety and enjoyment of life, a form of such wealth as we shall not see soon again. The period of individualism which formed the background of his art, giving the artist a full opportunity to develop his own personality to its utmost potentialities—this happy period is over. It was rudely ended by the World War.

The significance of this primary event, its spiritual meaning and effect, was of course not recognized at once. But the repercussions and emotional reactions were to be felt in art very soon.

The frightful experience of the war resulted in a flight from reality, and the artists who had lived through it now abandoned themselves to the impulses of their agitated sentiments. There first arose a huge wave of expressionism, producing strange works full of individualistic emotion, of passionate sentiment, of romantic ecstasy.

Even architecture, an art sternly material and therefore an art that does not easily succumb to the urge of self-expression, was seized by that wave of expressionism. Its tendencies are plainly reflected in such a romantic project, for instance, as Hans Poelzig's design for the Festspielhaus in Salzburg, a project in which reality is entirely neglected, even to the degree of destroying any possibility of practical execution. The design is the sheer product of an excessive fantasy, piling up large building masses, moving their walls and setting them swinging, dissolving all forms in a structure of dynamic lines that mocks the weight of matter as fantastically as any Baroque architecture could do. In fact, the project recalls in its eccentric fancy a design exactly two hundred years older: the façade for St. Sulpice in Paris, done by Juste-Aurèle Meissonier in 1726, a first bold experiment in introducing into architecture the new forms of the Rococo style which up to that time had only been used for interior decoration. While this experiment was kept from being realized by the French taste for the classic, Poelzig, on the other hand, was able to realize at least one of the outbursts of his exuberant imagination when he built the Grosse Schauspielhaus in Berlin, remodeling an old circus building into a theater for Max Reinhardt. The big auditorium is covered with a dome decorated with arches in stalactite forms, which hang far down into the room, improving the acoustic properties, concealing the sources of electric light, and also forming the triangular capitals of the columns: a strange piece of architecture, full of personal expression, and in its romantic attitude a characteristic product of this excited time.

Other examples of that urge for self-expression are the utopian designs of the German architect Bruno Taut, published in the first years after the war, and interesting for all time to come as documents illustrating the temper of this period. Condemned to involuntary leisure by the stagnation of building activity, the architect at his drawing-board plays with his roaming fancy. Aroused by the potentialities of modern building technique, thinking of its unlimited means not fully utilized as yet, he visualizes the coming of a world building master capable of shifting mountains. Sketching his vision in a series of lithographs, entitled *Alpine Architektur,* he anticipates the power of this super-builder, transforming the natural formations of geological development into architectural structures, dissolving mountain peaks into lofty and lambent turrets, and vaulting valleys with wide-spanned domes of glass, lighted by electric current and shining from inside like radiant crystals. Or take his other book, *The Earth as a Good Dwelling, or The Dissolution of Cities,* a product mainly of self-contemplation. Driven by his social consciousness, he thinks about the most urgent and actual problem of the time, how to get housing, how to change the earth into a pleasant abiding place worthy of mankind. In casual sketches dashed off with a pen, like short notes, not real projects intended to be carried out, but only a Utopia, he dreams of a better form of human settlement, freed from the avoidable burden of urban agglomeration, and shows the possibilities which might exist were there no obstacles or limitations to the pursuit of this high goal.

And the same line of self-expression is followed in the early projects of Erich Mendelsohn who by virtue of his alert intelligence and his strong and aggressive temperament soon became one of the most audacious members of the *avant-garde*. Take the Einstein Tower, for example, erected in Potsdam in 1920, an astronomical observatory, devoted to the great scholar for his studies on the nature of light. In this building Mendelsohn accomplished in a spectacular manner a sort of synthesis between Poelzig and van de Velde. The numerous commissions which soon came to him from the commercial and industrial world, strengthened him with their discipline, and led him happily out of the blind alley of expressionism.

THE YOUNG GENERATION

In fact, under the pressure of actual practice the younger generation soon came back to reality. Born between 1880 and 1890, this generation had its childhood and youth stamped with the realistic impress of a world-wide war that speeded up, by its ethical and spiritual tensions and repercussions, the rate of change. Judging from its works produced in the last two decades, this is an earnest generation seeking for fundamentals, accustomed to serve, and to subordinate itself to, a guiding idea. It has radically abjured the artistic individualism of its fathers. Indeed, it

PROJECT FOR THE FAÇADE
OF ST. SULPICE, Paris, 1726.
Juste-Aurèle Meissonier, architect

PROJECT FOR THE THEATRE OF MAX REINHARDT, Salzburg, 1924.
Hans Poelzig, architect

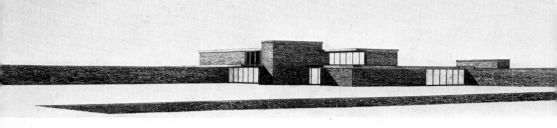

PROJECT FOR BRICK HOUSE, 1923. Mies van der Rohe, architect

HOUSE IN GUBEN, 1929. Mies van der Rohe, architect

seems to have lost in the bitterness of its hard youth all impulse for ornamental play. For the representatives of this generation, art no longer exists for its own sake, but is a constituent of active life. In order to restore art to its proper meaning, they demand the opportunity to relate it in organic order to life. Ready to limit the freedom of the artistic personality in the service of this super-personal need, they take a practical part in the necessary re-shaping of life, willingly attacking its manifold problems wherever they meet them in their own field. Grown up in the principles of thought whose direction is pointed and whose power is shown in the progressive transformations of our world, they try to re-establish the indispensable identity between life and art, between content and form. The essence of their aim was clearly expressed in the manifesto of the first International Congress for New Building at Geneva in 1928, proclaiming the plan of "uniting art with the structure of a new world."

THE INFLUENCE OF CUBISM

Now, to take up the thread of historical events: before the war the movement had come to a dead-end with its adventure in expressive ornaments. Now looking for a new track to proceed along, it chanced upon the ideas of cubism, that new European movement just arising in painting and sculpture. This chance most vigorously affected the new spirit of building, and urged it into a direction leading to results entirely different from the luxuriant forms of Frank Lloyd Wright, although there was full assent to his principles, and although it was, according to J. J. P. Oud, who ought to know, precisely the enthusiasm

147

aroused by Wright's form that to a large extent paved the way for cubism in architecture.

Cubism—that is one of the numerous currents in art originating from the reaction against impressionism. With it came the turn from the naturalistic picture to the stylized image, in short to a canon of style. Cubism traces its origin back to Cézanne, who tried to lead painting beyond the dissolving tendencies of impressionism to a higher development. His problem was figuration, was consolidation of the form. He sought the grand style, and devoted all his efforts in a life full of work to develop a new principle of form and order for painting. He studied nature, searching in her face for simple, elementary forms which could serve as elements of organization. In the way of his observations he discovered that "everything in nature is shaped according to sphere, cone and cylinder. Knowing how to paint according to these basic forms, one can later on do everything one wants to."

Of this personal theory, the school of cubism made an esthetic ideology, developing it into a new canonic doctrine of style, containing the principles of abstract painting divorced from a mere imitation of reality. Following Cézanne's discovery, cubism dissolves the appearance of things into their basic forms, it splits up the form into its component parts, and of the basic elements so gained, it organizes its abstract paintings into a compositional unit. As a product of purely speculative esthetics, the method may be as disputable as many of its results. With its fundamental idea, however, cubism points far ahead of the problematical results of its abstract figurations. This idea corresponds to a new

tendency of our time towards collective consciousness demanding a uniting symbol, a parabolical abstraction "embracing all
and everything." Cubism, aspiring toward the super-personal
form, the form of general validity, tends toward style. And with
this tendency, urging art out of its private sphere of personal
styles into a new collective style, therewith restoring to art its
public and social concern, cubism gave the movement for modern building a new momentum. Stimulated by this new style
idea and following its principles, it finally emerged from the
dead point it had reached after the vain efforts of the *Art Nouveau* movement.

With the rise of cubism, the artistic spirit turned again to the
idea of style. And cubism considered itself as the first step, and
its principles as the pace-maker for this style, no less in architecture than in painting and in sculpture. Cubism, declared
J. J. P. Oud, is to be regarded as a transitional state, in which
the old system is replaced by a new order. (And we will keep in
mind this interpretation given by the leading representative of
this new school.) Cubism in architecture means both resignation
and change. Resignation by conscious return to utmost simplicity, change by conscientious adjustment of building to the modern demands of use and to the present practice of life and work.
The cubistic school in architecture, striving to replace the mul-
tiplicity of forms by a new unity of form, goes back, for the
present, to the very elemental. Therefore the almost ascetic re-
serve, the puritanic abstinence from any ornament and from
any detail not immediately necessary; and therefore, on the other
hand, in order to compensate for this resignation, the decisive

149

devotion to technical progress and the concentrated interest in constructional problems. Following these principles, cubism created in architecture a new form-type which meanwhile gained an almost international validity.

CHARACTERISTICS OF THE NEW STYLE

To characterize in brief the attributes of this new form-type: the bulk of the building is broken up in parts, following cubistic principles, and the various parts by skillful grouping of the masses are then composed into a whole, in its aspect "still revealing the elements of the original analysis." To such a simplified form of geometrical character belongs the flat roof; it is the logical consequence of the esthetic principle of the style: the cubic blocks of the building mass and the even planes of its walls need a clear and sharp-edged contour. The loosening of the building bulk and the dynamic grouping of the masses afford by means of the resulting shadows all the molding desirable, and lead to a plain treatment of the façades which are consequently designed for graphic rather than for plastic effects. This explains the preference for smooth, white-colored plaster for covering the outer walls: it is favored because it emphasizes the intended effect by strengthening the black-white appearance. And this kind of surface treatment, showing no longer any joints, also serves to express the tendency toward dematerializing of the walls, the lightening of its mass and weight, and to articulate its new character as a mere skin, which it achieved with the adoption of modern skeleton construction. In the total aspect the graphic element prevails: line takes a decisive part and becomes once again the acknowledged leader of plastic form. The building mass, largely loosened and lightened, assumes the strength of its plastic effect through the interplay of large even planes and the clear flow and graduated dynamics of lines. Hence follows that striking similarity with the stylistic features which Wilhelm Pinder has given for the medieval sculpture of about 1400; and he himself has pointed to this stupendous parallel in the pursuits of modern art. "The eye of the spectator," he says, "should not take in the volume at once, but should rise with the lines along the contour. Everything tangible is transmuted, so to speak, to a lighter substance. The form becomes alive for the traveling rather than for the fixed glance. The eye is not offered single and separate main views, on the expansions of which it can rest; but it is kept in gliding motion, along the lines and contours of the figure." These features came to prominence in Wright's art, where we have found them developed to highest effectiveness. And after all, they are features not only of architectural composition, but also, as plainly proved by the paradigm of this master, characteristic of the change in the idea of structure, of the turn to organic planning.

In its aspect, and in full contrast to Wright's form, the new form-type is of intentional and elaborate simplicity. Its physiognomical expression is crabbed and severe, but with all the scantiness and even parsimony of the form, the type attains a certain solidity, and even elegance, through the careful treatment of construction, through the exactness and precision of the technical details. Endowed with inner control and outer coldness, filled with renunciation, the new form convinces through the ethic force of the style idea more than the sensuous effects of its artistic substance. The style idea always prevails, and the more the personality of the single artist steps back behind the general aims of the school, the more the character of the building appears impersonal.

With the rise of this style of cubism, the new spirit of building entered a new phase which up to now is also its latest one. The generative impulse of the new spirit is now no longer limited to the more or less interesting experiments of individuals. Diffusing itself ever wider, its ideas have penetrated everywhere: its sphere extends from Europe over the United States to the Far East. And the results of its work prove unmistakably the coherence of a world-wide school. The new spirit has now soared far beyond any special concern with the overthrow of historic forms. In its progress, it has coined elements of a new language, and although it may not yet be able to use that language for speaking in pure poetry, it has already changed the outward forms of our time.

THE INTERNATIONAL LEADERS

Among the great number of architects who share in the development of this new language, there are a few individualities whose work has gained international influence. The first place is due to J. J. P. Oud. Gifted with great artistic talents sustained by an intelligence of equal strength, he was predestined for the profession of architect. Born in 1890, he grew up in the ideas of Berlage who by means of purification had established a new discipline and integrity of form. To Oud, who was well acquainted with Berlage's theory, based on geometrical concepts, the ideas of cubism came as enlightenment, developing his self-consciousness. He joined a group of young painters connected by kindred views, and with Peter Mondrian and Theo van Doesburg, he founded a magazine, *De Stijl,* as a center for the development and interpetation of the theory and principles of the new style of cubism.

When he first came to practice, he was still under the commanding influence of Berlage, and in such buildings as the large apartment blocks for workmen, erected in a suburb of Rotterdam, he even surpassed the master in puritanism. The plain blocks, built in brick, present an exterior of an almost repellent coldness and austerity. Impelled by his fresh enthusiasm for the ideas of cubism, he then designed a series of projects demonstrating the theory of the style and so truly devoted to principles that they almost appear as products of academic sobriety. But from project to project he attained greater freedom, finally doing justice to his artistic talent, hitherto too much suppressed by the disciplining forces of his intellectuality. As architect of the city of Rotterdam, he built a few housing schemes, proving that his social responsibility and his respect for function is not infringed by his profound respect for pure form. His experiments in colored architecture prove not only his ability to overcome his early puritanism, but also his esthetic understanding of the functional meaning of color. In his buildings, however (and he has built all-too-few), he truly adheres to the principles of cubism, using no other form elements than cube, sphere and cylinder. He began with the simplest forms, strengthening his discipline by intentional primitiveness, and not before his latest work, a housing scheme in the Hook of Holland, did he advance to the use of the curve. Oud is extremely severe and straightforward with himself. And so is his form: chaste and severe, but always really finished, and filled with music and rhythm. And so his work gives both a summary of the stage of development and a measure of quality for the achievements the new spirit of building has reached up to now.

A congenial talent, and related to Oud in many respects, is Ludwig Mies van der Rohe. Born in 1886, he worked as a beginner in the atelier of Peter Behrens, whose great form and monumental style must have most nearly responded to the innate instinct of the youngster. Developing this instinct, he became a true guardian of the spirit of form, and thereby a leader in a generation which, by its tendency towards theory and principle as well as by its inclination to try the new potentialities of modern technique, is often enticed to one-sided occupation with the mere rationale of building. At the same time, however, Mies is devoted with all conviction to the new ideas of structure, and pursues their problems with a resolute radicalism not easily to be equaled.

He, too, approached the aims which direct the work of his generation by way of cubism. From this period of his development originated a project for a country house which as an exemplary work, demonstrating the ideas of the time in the most concentrated essence, gained among the young generation a fame that started a new experimental school. The significance of this project lies not only in the esthetic element, which in the bold dissolution of the building bulk and the plastic grouping of the single blocks, reduced to elemental geometric forms, clearly demonstrates the doctrine of cubism; it lies also, and even more, in the spiritual attitude of the project, manifesting the change in the idea of structure. Look, for instance, only at the ground plan. To be sure, it is fully based on a formal conception, and so close to the ideas of cubism that the design, eyed as a mere drawing, looks like the reproduction of one of Mondrian's paintings. Yet it also reveals the decisive transformations meanwhile achieved in the inner structure. The single rooms are no longer bound in themselves, any more than is the bulk of the building. As in Wright's most advanced examples of organic building, the boundaries of the rooms are loosened, their outer walls are fully opened, their volumes flow into one another, penetrate each other, and thereby achieve a connection more intimate than the mechanical one of geometric order, accomplished by the mere relation of axes.

The programmatic ideas of this project have been developed to the last consequences, and carried through with the full freedom of artistic maturity, in the House Tugendhat, erected in 1931 in Brno, Czechoslovakia. In this building, furthered by the favor of a large-minded and imperturbable client, trusting the virtues of his architect, the achievements of the new spirit are put to test in an extreme example: it almost looks like a demonstration project, designed for an exhibition. Yet so much is its technical radicalism—a detailed analysis is given in another chapter—imbued with artistic spirit that the building almost appears as a work of pure art.

155

Mies van der Rohe, too, has built very little. But he designed a series of fundamental projects in which he attacked the problem of the skyscraper, of the office building, of the workmen's apartment house and of the private dwelling house, each of these projects having the value of a typical solution. It is characteristic of his special talent, and not due to mere chance, that with the development of steel furniture the problem of cultivating and refining its form devolved upon him: it was he who created the technically adroit form of the tubular steel chair, that form in which this new industrial product has since conquered the world's markets.

A pupil of Peter Behrens' is Walter Gropius, born in 1883. From the beginning, he turned his manifold talents to one main task: to the development of new building types and new models for standardized production. He is fanatically devoted to the physical conditions of his problem, fulfilling with exceptional skill its economic, its technical and its formal needs. In 1919, when he was appointed, as successor of Henry van de Velde, to the direction of the School for Applied Arts in Weimar, he transformed that institution into the "Bauhaus," a school for technical education based on a modern program (transferred to Dessau in 1925). The object of the school was to train students in the various productive activities involved in building, and to educate a new type of craftsman, qualified for co-operating with industry and capable of developing for the machine-made product a new form, adapted to the technical process of production and revealing its specific character. The school was organized as a group of workshops, intended as laboratories, in which were developed models of objects for standardized production, models which in practical work and continued experiments were bettered and refined in form.

As an architect, Gropius himself experimented with new methods of construction, with new materials and techniques, always striving in his buildings for the final type that would express their function as well as the nature of their material substance. Such bold efforts at innovation are unavoidably made under varying chances, always running the risk of failing. Gropius had frequent opportunities to make this observation. But never discouraged, in spite of many enmities, he has followed his call, sticking to his ideas and convictions with tenacious self-denials.

Erich Mendelsohn has already been mentioned. Born in 1887, he came early to an extensive practice, and for many years was one of the most prolific architects of the young generation. He built a large number of office buildings, of department stores and factories all over Germany, he erected a large movie theater in Berlin; and attracted by these conspicuous achievements, the Soviets availed themselves of his unusual talent and gave him the commission for an important project for a large textile plant in Leningrad. After having yielded, as a youngster, to the temptations of expressionism, he undertook, in order to stimulate his talent, extended study trips to Holland, the birthplace of modern building, and to the United States, the native country of Frank Lloyd Wright and the motherland of large-scale construction, and finally, he also absorbed the ideas of cubism. These various impulses, however, were thoroughly thought out, and so entirely assimilated to his own conceptions that he finally succeeded in developing an individual style. These conceptions, however, were definitely determined by his urge toward self-expression, and so was his style: eloquent in its effect, filled with declamatory power, the form itself full of expressive movement. But this individual style, although it showed decisive preference for all sorts of modern materials and forms of construction, is not quite adequate to the spirit of the age in that it was too subjective and still contained too many romantic remainders and ostentatious personal elements.

LE CORBUSIER

As for Le Corbusier, he certainly enjoys the reputation of being the most eminent exponent of modern ideas: the passions of both the friends and adversaries of modern building are roused if only his name is mentioned. Born in 1888, in Chaux-de-Fonds, French Switzerland, he is a man of many accomplishments: a great artist and a brilliant draftsman, an original spirit and rationalistic thinker, and finally, like most Frenchmen, an excellent writer. And he also proves himself a true Frenchman by pushing his ideas to the extreme, putting his conclusions in the most striking and wittiest aperçus, as illuminating as sharply pointed. "Due to the machine," he said, "our environment is undergoing a comprehensive transformation, in its outer aspect as well as in its utilization. We have acquired a new vision and a new social life, but to that transformation we have not yet adapted building." And he decided to devote his life to the task of adapting art to the changing environment.

FROM PERSONAL EXPRESSION TOWARDS A NEW STYLE

Le Corbusier, the architect, is the reincarnation of the painter Charles-Edouard Jeanneret. And in this reincarnation, he still preserves his glowing admiration for painting, which, as he asserts, has first effected, since the rise of cubism, full contact with the changed environment, outdoing all other arts. And cubism is one element of his style, modern technique the other. In modern technique and its constructive spirit tending toward synthesis, Le Corbusier sees the driving forces dominating the age and determining its style. And modern technique, conferring upon the artist enhanced freedom of mobility, made possible for him the daring adventure of realizing his cubistic visions in the three-dimensional forms of architecture.

It indicates the character of these visions that his buildings have been described as lyric poems in glass and steel. Indeed, his structures seem to be altogether freed from every material weight, from the force of gravity itself. Cubes of air penetrate their entirely open masses; large areas of glass increase their transparency. Some of his houses are raised above the ground on stilts, so that they stand in the air, and under the house the garden, continuing on the level of the ground-floor, is worked into a sort of terrace. In some of these houses, the interior is developed, like a studio, showing one single room the unit of which is divided into a great number of sections, varying in form and size, not separated from, but flowing into each other, and demarcated only by low partition walls or curved screens. And an immense apparatus of straight or winding stairways, of ramps, of platforms and corridors, projected like balconies, is used through the various stories in order to accomplish the necessary connection between these loose room sections. With a free hand, the architect takes the most daring risks, but with his artistic skill and assurance he always succeeds in developing a form which by its esthetic charm persuades even when it does not rationally convince.

It is a sort of cubistic stage setting, inspired perhaps by Meyerhold's "Unbounded Theater," that is accomplished in these buildings; and in his numerous designs and, perhaps at best, in his delightful and gracefully improvised pen sketches, he has dealt with this theme in ever novel variations. The most daring examples of his playful fancy, exhibiting all sides of his easy talent, are given in such buildings as the Villa de Monzie in Garches, near Paris, and in the Villa Savoye, at Poissy (1929). These houses display all the varieties of his effective art of architectural *mise-en-scène,* up to the roof-garden where platforms and outlooks are erected in forms recalling the bridge of an ocean steamer. Indeed, every perspective in these houses is arranged to the effect of a cubistic painting, including the view into the landscape offered from the roof-garden and so elaborately cut into sections by the open framework of the concrete screens and piers and beams that their geometric forms become an integral part of the picture.

In each of his numerous manifestoes, Le Corbusier explains modern building as a problem of functional structure. But to draw conclusions from his practical achievements, he himself seems to be interested not so much in *building* as a structural problem as in Architecture, supposed to be, according to his own definition, "a thing of art, a phenomenon of poetic emotion."

August Perret, his teacher, though still using in his designs the classical detail, already showed more respect for the structural problems of building, and made an honest attempt towards an architectural interpretation of modern concrete construction when in 1922 he built the little Church of Notre Dame, Le Raincy, near Paris. And Eugène Freyssinet, the boldest among the modern building-engineers of France, in another effort to interpret modern construction, created a new form when he built the airship shed at Orley, near Paris, in 1916: a parabolically curved vault with ribs of thin-shelled concrete pipes, an utilitarian structure of purest beauty. Le Corbusier, however, the Picasso of modern architecture, deals not with the structural problem of building, but with the esthetic problem of an architectural style. And he uses modern construction mainly for its emotional power of expression.

But when the idea of style prevails, form always precedes function. It characterizes Le Corbusier's attitude towards the problem of structure that in his *Trois Rappels à M. les Architectes* he deals, first of all, with the plastic form, and that he next speaks of the surface, recommending for its arrangement the "regulating line," the old and approved expedient of academic composition. And only in the third place, he comes to the plan, although he always calls it "the generator." Corbusier, the theorist, declares the plan proceeds from within to without; Corbusier, the architect, however, is always ready to make in his ground plans far-going concessions, at the cost of function, in favor of the exterior. And while Corbusier accused academicism of having made the ground plan into a work of graphic art, ex-

161

hibiting an ornament of radiant stars, his own ground plans with their elaborate interplay of straight and oblique lines, of curves and spirals, almost recalling the abstract paintings of Picasso, are certainly no less ornamental. Thus, for all his radicalism, Corbusier in his conception is not so far from those adversaries whom he antagonizes most: from the academicians.

As a matter of fact, with his radicalism Le Corbusier has thoroughly overthrown the traditional doctrine of academicism, but only with the result of replacing it with another, no less abstract principle, with the doctrine of cubism. In architecture, however, cubism means rather a return to elementary geometry than a turn towards organic order. Nothing, indeed, could be more dangerous for the new spirit of building, so long as its ideas are not yet fully ripened, than a premature lapse into doctrine. The lesson of History gives warning: even in earlier times, French radicalism, "a mixture of emotion and logic, one-sidedly tending towards program, system and doctrine," has stifled by its urge toward systematization the hopeful beginnings of an organic style. It was the radical spirit of the French Gothic that nipped the development of the Romanesque style in the bud. The French Gothic absorbed the structural ideas of the Romanesque style, before they developed into full maturity, and forcing them up to the extreme in a rationalistic system of construction, condensed their essentials into a logical scheme. Convincing, through the overpowering effects of its logical formalism, French Gothic carried the day by its radical spirit and unified the system into a classical rule.

And once again it is French radicalism that has reduced the

BAUHAUS SCHOOL, Dessau, Germany, 1925-1926. Walter Gropius, architect

BAUHAUS SCHOOL WORKSHOPS

(Courtesy Department of Architecture, Museum of Modern Art, New York)

HOUSE IN GARCHES near Paris, 1927-1928. Le Corbusier, architect

HOUSE IN SWITZERLAND, 1925. Le Corbusier, architect

(Courtesy Department of Architecture, Museum of Modern Art, New York)

ideas of modern building to the common denominator of the classical rule. In the command of these rules Le Corbusier proves his esthetic mastery. His work, infused with the spirit of Geometry as the source of its order, certainly affords us "the sublime satisfactions of Mathematics which gives us such a grateful perception of order." And demonstrating in his achievements this spirit of order, he may convince us as artist, but he cannot convert us to belief that it is just the spirit of Geometry which determines the modern mode of thinking and affords the universal law under which our time is striving for a new order. And eyes which do see realize that the creations of modern technique which excite Le Corbusier's highest admiration have not originated from mathematical calculation alone; the machine, the automobile, the airplane, are typical creations of organic structure, and what they look like they really are—products based on the evolutionary laws of organic nature.

It is by the predominance of the style idea involved in the universal law of Geometry that Le Corbusier's buildings are prevented from obtaining that individuality of character so happily displayed in every work of Frank Lloyd Wright. Indeed, Le Corbusier, *l'homme géometrique,* is in every respect the antithesis and antagonist of Wright. Le Corbusier's art is based on an experience of Education, that of Wright on an experience of Nature. Le Corbusier's art is sophisticated and decidedly intellectual, and it is founded on a principle of structure created by reason, not on the elementary laws of organic growth. His art is predominantly urban, that of Wright emphatically rural. Wright's houses are built in complete harmony with their surroundings, Le Corbusier's buildings are built against nature, having no contact with their surroundings, and knowing even the landscape only in the artificial form of roof-gardens and terraces.

Only in the negative there exists a parallel: Wright's art, in the luxuriance of its form, is too one-sidedly devoted to the needs of a small upper class; while the social conception on which Le Corbusier's art is based fits exclusively the habits of life characteristic of a certain group of metropolitan intellectuals. A great admirer of the metropolis himself, he has devoted a series of studies to its problems. It is characteristic of his conception of this problem that he declares speed to be, above all, the special and most important feature of the modern city. And in the plans advanced for the solution, he consequently declares the level site as best suited for the modern metropolis, and repudiates the natural amenities of the hilly site just for the sake of such an abstract thing as speed. He even scorns the stimulating effects of a waterfront: the river, he says, flows far away from the city. So in his plans he provides for a scheme of wide, straight streets which the automobile can follow at high speed, and of skyscraper apartments equipped for a pleasant life of a club-like style. Located on wide squares and surrounded with large open spaces, these lofty towers, bathed in light and air, afford the clear contours of the pure forms of Geometry, needed as compositional elements to give the city its architectural form. Indeed, "architecture" triumphs again, and the social and economic problem of the city remains unsolved.

The art of Le Corbusier is revolutionary without being new,

that of Wright is new, although it is not revolutionary. In Le Corbusier's challenging book *Towards a New Architecture,* the old gods rise up again: Egypt, Byzantium, Rome, Michelangelo. Wright, on the contrary, feels a deep hatred for the Renaissance and always shows his contempt for it. His passionate love is directed toward those buildings, "which arose out of actual need," as he says, and which are fitted to their surroundings, built by men who knew "no other way than to make them fit these surroundings with true feeling. Buildings which arose like folksongs, and which are more worth while to study than all the self-conscious experiments of academic beauty." And as the nature of the problem which the modern movement for a century has endeavored to solve is programmatically defined in the two opposite terms "Architecture" and "Building," the question of its future development simply reads "Corbusier or Wright?"

In fact, with Corbusier and the establishment of cubism as a new style, the spirit of modern building has arrived at a critical turning point. To be sure, cubism has been received as an esthetic principle, and as such it has served to discipline the feeling for form, as well as to purify and solidify the form itself. But, being limited to the primary elements of Geometry, this style of cubism must soon exhaust its formal possibilities; and so tending towards sterility, it must develop, and already has in many cases, into a new academicism which, although it suggests in its aspect a radical modernism, is not better than its conservative predecessor. If the new style of cubism turns out not to be what it originally was supposed to be, namely a transitory stage in the development of the movement, then instead of introducing the rise of a new order, it will only stabilize the authority of the geometric doctrine. As a matter of fact, the spirit of modern building was closer to its structural problem with the principles of the *Art Nouveau* movement and its much defamed and so often misintepreted ornament than with the ideas of cubism, which with its esthetic doctrine arrests the growth of the form in its development toward the organic.

2. TECHNIQUE, CONSTRUCTION, AND FORM

In a book on modern building, one cannot well omit a chapter on the new building methods derived from modern technique, and their influence on form. As a matter of fact, modern building owes a great debt to modern technique. With steel and concrete, technical genius has given to building two new materials which have not only changed the basic methods of construction, but by increasing the physical strength of building have also enhanced its structural potentialities. To mention only one of these new potentialities, perhaps not the most important, but in its effects certainly the most obvious: thanks to the new methods of steel and concrete construction, building has been able to outgrow its former limits of size, and in this regard has, so to speak, finally freed itself of all bondage. These new methods of construction enable building to span the widest voids and to produce rooms of nearly unlimited dimensions without the use of supporting posts.

The new methods of construction, however, not only enlarged the possibilities of building, but also changed the character of structure in principle, thereby bringing about a complete spiritual revolution in building. A revolution probably no less radical and decisive in its effects than the basic change of conception that took place in medieval architecture after the pointed arch and the ribbed vault had been invented. A revolution which involved, as it did in Gothic, a large number of new problems of form.

Interpreting these revolutionary methods of modern construction in the scientific terms of Statics, one may say that modern construction brought about a transition from the inflexible to the flexible, from the stiff to the elastic methods of building. As to its nature, modern construction is framework, related in its principle to the traditional timber framework, but in a higher stage of development, with a much more refined utilization of the technical resources. It separates the organism of the building into organs of different functions: the active organs supposed to do the supporting work, and the passive organs serving only for space enclosure. When in common usage a modern steel frame construction is called a skeleton, language accurately discerns with such a term the organic character of the structure.

One of the main advantages derived from this new method of construction is the complete freedom gained for the arrangement of the ground plan. The distribution of the rooms is completely independent of the relation to supporting walls, formerly enforced by constructive necessities. The wall itself, freed from its former function of support, loses in bulk and weight, and in its tendency towards lightness and thinness, it finally acquires the nature of a mere skin: an inner partition wall possibly as thin as a membrane; as covering outer skin, transparent or non-transparent—wind-*eye* and wind protection at the same time. The wall openings are widened, the windows turn into glass walls, the whole building bulk loosens up, and there results a structure of floating lightness which seems almost entirely freed from the force of gravity.

MODERN BUILDING NOT A PASSIVE PRODUCT OF TECHNIQUE

To be sure, modern construction responds readily to the ideas of organic structure, and is an obedient tool for realizing the principles of order followed by the new spirit of building. Hence, it is a common opinion, repeated again and again, that modern building is a result, or a downright product, of modern technique. And this widely current but still untenable opinion implies enthusiastic praise to some, moral indignation to others. Certain though it may be that modern technique is one of the most important and strongest components of new building, it is nevertheless quite erroneous to assume that modern construction will produce of itself, somewhat in the way of cause and effect, the new forms of architecture. There are enough modern buildings which plainly disprove such an assumption. In their erection extensive use is made of modern methods of construction and of new building materials, but from their outer appearance nobody would ever realize the character of this construction. The structure is covered with a rich drapery of historical styles the forms of which are not only contrary to the nature of the modern construction, but indeed often impair its efficiency. Under cover of this historical dress nothing of the powerful effect spreading from the bare structure is to be perceived. In fact, these buildings are, as it was said of the goddess Aphrodite, more powerful naked than clad.

FORMAL INTERPRETATION OF THE NEW CONSTRUCTION

Although the new construction does not produce the new architectural form of itself, it is based on a distinct principle of structure that decisively needed to be followed in developing the architectural form. And in so far we may say that the architectural form is inherent and latently included in the construction itself. And it is of the greatest interest, indeed, to study how the modern architect deals with these new form problems involved in modern construction, how he tries to interpret its character by an expressive form appealing to emotion.

In this way, through translating the nature of modern construction into a new means of architectural expression, have arisen all the new and well-known forms which characterize modern building. Take, for instance, that striking wall-pattern dividing the façade into long horizontal strips of spandrels and glass areas, generally used for modern office buildings and department stores. It has been derived from modern cantilever construction where the vertical columns of the skeleton are set back from the front, inside the building. From the nature of this construction, freeing the outer walls from all supporting members, there is developed a new architectural form, making visible the changed function of the wall as a mere shell, in a pattern consisting of continuous strips alternately transparent and opaque. And this new pattern, first essayed in 1922 by Mies van der Rohe in a study project for an office building, gives to the façade a strong effect by the continuous flow of the horizontal lines which guide the eye in rapid flight along the building.

Modern construction has also bestowed upon building the technical possibilities of free suspension, and this new feature has been developed into architectural forms that give to building the fantastic effect of floating. Floating, by the way, is a function limited to organisms, and as a function of building, it was unknown, indeed, to classic architecture, based as that was on the static laws of Geometry. Elevated above the ground level, without any visible base, the building seems to be suspended in the air, demonstrating a new lightness of its masses. That it does not need any external piers or stilts, that it supports itself, is by intuition not to be reconciled with the laws of gravity. These laws, however, are repealed by the inner strength of the construction, by the elastic force of steel, acting invisibly. This amazing process, made possible with the progressive conquest of nature by the human mind, excites the play of the imagination. And making it an object of artistic representation, creative imagination transforms this process into a new architectural form, convincing the eye through the authenticity of its appearance.

It is, indeed, the nature of modern construction, characterized by its elastic structure, that with it the natural statics and its laws of load and support, gained from immediate experience of the human body, have been overcome to the benefit of a rationalistic domination of matter. It is worth mentioning that just this spiritual domination of matter and the turning away from the natural truth of experience and intuition have been declared to be the aim and characteristic of expressionism in architecture. Indeed, this aim is discernible, as it was in Gothic, which denied with the greatest consequence this natural truth of experience. With the achievement of modern technique, there have been developed new forms, which "though they appear of a quite rationalistic nature, a pure objectification in the material, plainly prove their purely spiritual origin." And just from its strict objectivity regarding the principles of structure the new form acquires its fantastic features. As George Dehio has said of the Gothic: "As construction it is full of the most ingenious rationalism, but only in the reality of construction; in appearance, it looks quite irrationalistic, that is to say subdued to a higher than earthly causality."

CONSTRUCTIVISM

The modern architect feels a naïve pleasure in the new technical acquisitions, and sometimes he is obviously carried away by the possibilities of modern building technique and by the expressiveness of modern building materials. This enthusiasm, as may be easily understood, occasionally leads to exaggerations. On one hand, the esthetic charms of the materials are misused for simply decorative effects; on the other, the technical innovations are overemphasized: in both cases the value of the material is overrated to the detriment of the esthetic substance of the form. It may be true to the purpose to fill the interior of a workshop, or a factory, with light by complete dissolution of the outer walls in glass. It may also be desirable to enlarge the window-openings in our houses to give the interior close contact with surrounding nature. The extent to which building has meanwhile been affected by this sound tendency, is to be seen from estimates, published in Robert S. Lynd's study on Middletown, according to which the majority of houses, constructed in the last ten or fifteen years, have at least fifty per cent more glass surface than in 1890. But in many a modern house the use of glass seems to be taken as a point of honor, as an article of faith, so to speak, the credo being to enlarge the area of the window-openings to the utmost. Such exaggerations grow only from the wish to revel in technical novelties and to boast of the charm of new materials. What Le Corbusier said is true: that a window may as well be three hundred feet as three feet wide. But it becomes pure dogmatism when the real demands of function are sacrificed to the theory; for then it is no better than the aimless insistence on the use of axes in academic architecture. A kind of esthetic constructivism exists in modern building, composing with the elements of modern construction and machinery in the same way that academic architecture composes with columns and cornices. The works of this modern romanticism of the machine do not lack a sensational effect, but still this effect, as in all sorts of academic composition, is of a merely decorative character, and does not rest on truth of artistic form.

There is also to be found in modern building a sort of primitive constructivism. Impressed by the emotional effect spreading from the bare structure, many an architect takes mere construction to be the same as architectural form. Construction, however, is an end in itself only for the engineer; for the architect it is still a raw material to be molded and brought into architectural form. When, however, the process of transforming the structure from the sphere of mere technique to the sphere of art has not yet begun, or remains unfinished, the work of the architect gets stuck in the material. And as architectural form, it lacks the emotional appeal which the construction affords.

The esthetic value attributed in our time to the pure form of use must not eclipse the fundamental truth that the sphere of Technique is separate from that of Art. To be sure, the pure form of use is existent in both spheres, and grows in each. But it can only develop into a work of art if it is elevated by the creative spirit to a sphere where necessity becomes freedom, where form follows the rules of reason but keeps its meaning beyond all reason and, freed from the idea of use and purpose, appeals to the senses and the emotions alone by its form.

LACK OF ORNAMENT

Modern building, on its way toward a definite form, is very likely to develop a sort of technical style, a style which accepts, both practically and imaginatively, the qualities inherent in materials; a style which consciously utilizes for its forms the cultivated beauty of the finished materials, the visual surface values of steel, glass, ceramics, and so forth; values achieved by an intensive process of technical refinement. Modern building, since it relies on the work of machine and industrial technique rather than on the work of craftsmen, cannot have ornament. But what it loses in this respect, it regains many fold by the charm and expressiveness inherent in its refined materials, the exactitude of its technique, and the precision of its forms. As an essential product of our time and as a truthful expression of modern life, modern building, it has to be granted, will probably not look otherwise than our machines, our airplanes and automobiles. It will not be more pleasant in its features, more poetic or romantic in its emotional effect. But modern building will also be no less intuitive, original, and imaginative than the works and forms of modern technique: it will be another, and a no less admirable, emanation of the human creative instinct. And in its best works, modern building will equal the architectural achievements of the past. Based on a principle of order that takes the structure as an organism, its works, fully adapted to function and environment, will once more embrace life as a whole.

3. NEW BUILDING TYPES

ON THE NATURE OF THE TYPE

The ideas of modern building, at the beginning of the nineteenth century only an inspiration, have now grown into realization. The new spirit has meanwhile created a great number of new building types, proving the strength as well as the limits of its generative power.

These types have not arisen as individual creations of a single architect. The type is the final product of a common creative process, continued through generations and shared in by current customs and habits of life, by the economic forces of the age and its technical potentialities, as well as by the formative skill of many architects. Now, in times in which a constant order prevails and life runs its steady course in fixed paths, the architect finds his work well prepared, his task well outlined: for the part he has to contribute to that creative process, he is directed by the guiding star of living traditions. From the constancy of the time and the established authority of its social order, there results a definite uniformity of demands from which gradually derive traditional building types of general validity. The persistence of these traditional types forms the primary prerequisite for the architect, if he is to devote all his strength to the potentialities of his individual talents. The architect is the child as

176

well as the father of order. And as every one of his creations is a child of that order by which he himself is nourished, so his creative forces can only be developed to full freedom when he is bound to a constant order. This freedom, then, he will utilize as an artist, refining and modifying the traditional building types he finds before him. Many such modifications are conceivable, made obligatory by varying climatic and geographical conditions, by local requirements of life habits and building traditions. To these manifold variations of the traditional types we owe, for instance, that inexhaustible wealth and unlimited variety of architectural physiognomy peculiar to the medieval town.

To the modern architect, the opportunity is denied of working under the fostering favor of an authoritarian and firmly established order. Living at the borderline between two eras, he is faced with the problematical conditions derived from a total crisis of order. And owing to the uncertain character of the times, the task of the architect is not only difficult, it is indeed in many cases beyond practical possibility of a final solution.

In every range in the broad field of his activities, he stumbles over the obstacles put in his way by an unsettled age. In every task set for him by the various institutions of society, by church, school and family, he runs up against a confusing array of problems, embarrassing him and taking up his time, and yet beyond his power to solve. These problems must be settled before his proper work can begin with good prospects of success. If, for example, a new school is to be planned, he is immediately faced with the general problems of education; and so long as a new conception for training the youth, so urgently needed in present times, has not been fully developed, how is he to arrive at a solution that will stand the test? And how can we expect from the architect that he plan for a new type of dwelling, when no conclusive agreement has yet been reached on the basic questions of living habits, of housing needs, of city organization?

In a work on Protestant church building, recently published in Germany, reference is made to the conflicting demands arising from the lack of liturgical unity. It characterizes the precise reverse of the normal conditions that in this book it was counted as one of the responsibilities of the architect to become himself a builder of the ritual by his decisions on details of planning!

At the present time, the whole substance, content, and basis of the architect's work is in a state of ferment. And so, as a matter of fact, he can accomplish his work only by making himself "the point of intersection of the various social forces" which define his task. In the analysis of these forces, however, and in the investigation of the often vaguely realized needs, he dissipates his own strength. The architect of today has to be economist and sociologist, artist and organizer in one person, and yet in many cases he succeeds only in getting stuck at the experimental stage and in reaching scarcely more than temporary solutions. But what is an artist to do who is possessed, as was the already quoted letter-writer of Dostoevsky's novel *Raw Youth,* by a longing for the present? "To guess . . . and make mistakes."

And therewith also a standard is given for the appraising of the works achieved in the meantime in modern building. They are experiments, often very crude and still in a raw state, stages

DEPARTMENT STORE, Rotterdam, 1928. Willem Marinus Dudok, architect

(Courtesy, School of Architecture Library, Harvard University)

CITY HALL, Hilversum, 1924. Willem Marinus Dudok, architect

VIEWS OF DE LA WARR PAVILION, Bexhill-on-Sea, England. Mendelsohn and Chermayeff, architects

(Courtesy Department of Architecture, Museum of Modern Art, New York)

on the way toward the finding of new types, and important for the manner in which they formulate problems rather than for the esthetic nature of their temporary solutions.

DISQUALIFICATION FOR THE MONUMENTAL

Now, as to the results of these manifold efforts toward developing new building types, the experiments, of course, have been furthest advanced, almost to a definite solution, in all those tasks where the architect has been faced with a clear program of demands, precisely defining the use and purpose for which the building is thought of; that is to say in such types as factories, office buildings, department stores and all those projects which need for their solution a sturdy and resolved realism.

On the other hand, these attempts have been, if not a total failure, at any rate not successful, with those types of building which by nature and destination need a monumental character. There have been in church architecture, for instance, many experiments towards modernizing the traditional types. Religion, however, is no longer what it once was, namely the center of everybody's life and conceptions, and the church no longer affords its sublime consolations in response to needs common to the entire community. And so the modernism of present-day church architecture, not inspired from within by a new religious spirit, appears to be a rather irrelevant demonstration, limited to the outer aspect and consisting merely in the application of modern methods of construction and building materials, such as steel, concrete and glass. An illuminating light on the situation is thrown when a new church, built in Düsseldorf in 1926 by

Otto Bartning, and making conspicuous use of all the processes and materials of modern technique, is called the "Steel Church," whereas in former times all churches used to be called by the names of saints. Most of these modern church buildings show a lack of appeal to religious feelings, and it proves the inadequate character of the new type, when the man in the street with his sound critical instinct responds to the effect of the new Church of St. Anthony in Basle, built in concrete and erected in 1926 by Karl Moser, by calling it a "Silo for Souls."

As a matter of fact modern building demonstrates a lack of sense for monumentality, and the same is true of present-day sculpture. But to be just, this lack is to be charged not to the impotence of modern art, but rather to the general spirit of the age. All monumental art is in the nature of a symbol, expressing, representing or recalling in its forms common ideas or conceptions of general consent, and therefore understood by everybody. Such great goods, however, are not granted to an age that lives through a crisis of all thought and social order. In the present there is, indeed, not any one idea, be it in politics, in economics or in art, that has won common consent.

This situation was clearly, and in an almost pathetic way, illuminated when Heinrich Tessenow built the War Memorial in Berlin, in 1931, if not the most successful, certainly the most honest attempt towards a solution of this difficult and in our time so ungrateful problem. In a large square hall which gets its light through a circular opening in the ceiling, he erected a simple square block of granite stone with a wreath of oak leaves, made of bronze, on its top. The interior is of the utmost possible simplicity, because for us only the very simple is the very true. The effect of the Memorial Hall is as strong as severe. When the building was finished, this effect was felt in governmental circles as not affording that sort of emotional appeal to which they were accustomed, and the architect, strictly rejecting the proposal that he add some adornment, was finally asked whether he would agree upon an inscription for adorning the walls. "Gentlemen," he answered, "I am ready to compromise, if you can find a text of a unifying character for that inscription." The gentlemen went to work, turning about the Bible and the works of the heroes of German literature, but they did not succeed in finding a single sentence, which was not apt to rouse the flaming protest of one or the other side. The inscription finally chosen for the memorial, had to be limited to a few abstract figures, to a common symbol, indeed, exonerated from any disrupting potentialities and beyond the reach of diverging opinions. It simply reads "1914-1918."

It is, in fact, the general spirit of the age which is not capable of, and what is more, not even longing for, the monumental. This strange phenomenon had already been observed by Karl Friedrich Schinkel more than a century ago. In an attempt to interpret his observations made on a journey to England, he wrote the following note: "The new time takes everything easy. There is no longer any belief in the absolute. And having realized too clearly the perishableness of all nature, we know that everything is soon going to change its structure. And so has been lost the sense for the monument." Besides this psychological reason, however, there is still another and even stronger one of a sociological nature, related to the change of society from an aristocratic to a democratic order. Whereas an aristocratic society indulges in erecting all kinds of monuments, using them as symbols to impress on the people the static character of the social building, a democratic society whose structure, based on the concept of organic order, is of dynamic character has no use, and therefore no desire, for the monument. Be that as it may, Schinkel's statement has been proved true by the facts: since it was written, almost no monument has been erected that by its artistic qualities stands the test.

A NEW TYPE OF DWELLING HOUSE

The more life is understood as an organic process, the more we strive to live it in accordance with its laws. This new attitude which is inducing a total change of our environment, is perhaps most clearly to be seen in the new demands raised in the sphere of domestic life—demands which by their persistence have meanwhile given rise to a new type of dwelling house.

It is not so long ago that the Villa was still in vogue, that questionable type of house, in which the new bourgeoisie of the nineteenth century saw its ideal of domestic building. This house was a bastard child of the *Maison de Plaisance,* developed by French classicism and spread in countless variations over the whole civilized world. The type was created to satisfy the demands of a mode of life entirely absorbed in social display. In the strong conventionality of its arrangement, this house reflects the solemn ceremony to which society subjugated its life from the hour of the *lever* to the small hours of the morning.

SCHOOL BUILDING, Groningen, Holland. L. C. van der Vlught, architect, and Wiebenga, engineer

SCHOOL BUILDING, Schneidemuehl, Germany
(*Courtesy Preussische Hochbauverwaltung, Berlin*)

TOBACCO FACTORY, Rotterdam. J. A. Brinckman and L. C. van der Vlught, architects. The construction view shows how the vertical columns are set back from the front. The outer wall is entirely freed from all supporting members and developed into a mere skin, the façade showing a pattern of long horizontal strips of spandrels and glass.

Around a co-ordinate system of axes, the rooms of the house were so arranged that the plan formed a geometric figure of regular contour and strict symmetry. And these rooms each of which formed a regular geometric figure, too, were so arranged side by side, with their doors all placed in a line, as to form an *enfilade,* opening an effective vista through the whole length of the house. With masterly art, the whole plan hangs together on a branched network of axes. Their ceremonial play continues even in the garden, and everywhere unfolds the full effect of its linear impetus. And in that masterly distribution, this type of house attained the final goal of its artistic ambition. The house— its plan forming an ornament in itself—was created to be an ornament to social life, the most conspicuous of many. No wonder that its form retained its lure, and became for the rising bourgeoisie the admired exponent of perfect housing culture. But as a mere pattern, imitated long after the society that had given it meaning had ceased to exist, its form degenerated more and more, finally developing into that mixed type of the nineteenth-century villa: a hideous house, which for the purpose of social display sacrificed the whole area of the ground floor, putting the kitchen with all the other economic rooms down in the basement; an arrangement not only detrimental to the efficiency of housekeeping, but also spoiling the comforts of domestic life by separating the ground floor from the garden level.

It is due to the new habits of life that this questionable type of house has meanwhile died out. The style of life has entirely changed in our time, and with it the type of our houses. We live as informally as our parents lived conventionally. We regard

183

the house as an efficient instrument for living a natural life and not, like our forebears, as an ornament for social display to be paid for with no matter how many inconveniences.

The diminished desire for social display reacted upon the house, first, with a decrease in the demand for purely formal spaciousness. Less room is needed, also, since in the modern economic system, working place and dwelling place have been definitely separated: one works downtown in the city but lives in a suburb. Moreover, the lives of the family's members are for a good part of the day spent outside of the home. This is a general rule for the man; it is in many cases true for his wife, too, as far as she is induced, by necessity or vocation, to practice a profession; it is particularly true for the children who with the extended system of public education are for many hours detained in school, at the playing field or in their youth organizations. Thus, in the modern house the dwelling space has been greatly reduced as to both the total number of rooms and their dimensions.

This tendency towards reducing the living space, so characteristic of our times, cannot be explained on economic grounds alone, though the vexatious problem of keeping servants, sharply felt in many households, has certainly increased the desire for simplifying the work of housekeeping. It cannot be questioned that this new tendency also reveals the influences of a new feeling for life, derived from the enhanced mobility gained by modern man. Bent on his new freedom for moving around, made possible by the spread of the automobile, he feels the excessive extent of his permanent residence as a constraint to settling down, and therefore as a burden rather than as comfort. Putting the consequences to be drawn from these connections in a pointed form, one may venture to say that it is the modern type of hotel room which represents, and this is particularly true for the United States, the dwelling demand of modern man in the most condensed form. In its highly developed comfort, in the completeness of its technical equipment, and in its elaborate fitting strictly limited to the necessary, this type affords, indeed, everything to satisfy modern dwelling demands—except the representation of personal taste.

The restriction as to the extent of dwelling space is compensated, on the other hand, by increased demands for efficiency, guaranteeing by an elaborate organization of the ground plan a far-reaching simplification of household work and a smooth and frictionless flow of domestic life. It is this enhanced demand for efficiency which in the modern house has led to the progressive specialization of the rooms. In the seventeenth century, the bedroom, to infer from its furniture, was at the same time living- and dining-room, dressing chamber and reception room. The modern house provides single rooms for each of these purposes; and a further division and differentiation of the rooms has occurred all over the house: a development which corresponds to the principles of modern technique, according to which the increase of efficiency is sought through functional division of labor. The improvement of quality in modern technics, said Wilhelm Ostwald, is attained through a process which is also denoted in living organisms as a characteristic and a measure of progress: that is through the distribution of the different functions to specialized organs. In this sense the modern house satisfies the increased demands for efficiency by differentiating its organism and assigning the various functions of domestic life, such as working, eating, cooking, sleeping, to separate and particularly specialized organs.

With this change of its organization, the modern house gained many times in comfort what it lost in grandeur. Private houses of palatial dimensions are left to us only as historical monuments; and when they are still to be met in present times, their owners almost always prove to be loaded with historical reminiscences. Living accommodations of such an extent as the ruler of Versailles once conceived as the type of shelter suitable to his rank, are hardly thinkable today. But we also read that sometimes the smoke of the fireplaces disturbed his repose in the sumptuous rooms, and that their pompous luxury did not save Le Roi Soleil from occasionally having his wine served frozen on the table. Due to the advances of technique, we are spared such inconveniences in our modest and limited dwellings. And when we speak today of luxury in a dwelling, a new connotation is given to the word. It does not mean a vast extent of dwelling space, but the increased comfort obtained by the more ample technical equipment.

The rapid increase in such equipment was shown in a series of interesting sketches suggested by the late Henry Wright and published in the *Journal of the American Institute of Architects* in 1922. These sketches follow the historical development from the dwelling of the first American colonists, which consisted of only two rooms and an open fireplace, up to the house of the present, which, with the increasing use of the oil furnace is definitely ridding itself of the unavoidable dirt connected with the use of coal. Electric current is used for every type of household work, for cooking as well as for cleaning and washing. And a great number of electrical appliances has been introduced for saving labor in the management of the home. Finally with the radio, the latest addition, the modern house has gained a new and highly sensitive organ, enabling it to catch the voice of the world.

Another aspect of the modern style of life is the great regard for all sorts of sport, and the emphasis on bodily hygiene. These characteristics of our mode of life are also expressed in the new type of domestic building. Modern man wishes to enjoy in his house the benefits of an outdoor existence. He disdains the padded comfort and the somber atmosphere of Victorian parlors. He does not care for the narrow apertures toward the outside; he demands bright rooms, filled wth light and air. In short, he asks, perhaps as compensation for the dehumanizing anomaly of a mechanized life, for a type of house that opens itself on all sides and also on its roof to the stimulating and regenerative virtues of nature.

To these demands the modern house responds with its wide-opening windows, its large terraces and roof gardens, generally known as the most characteristic and most popular features of its exterior. And it responds to them, also, with an organization of its interior which, based on the principles of organic order, in its aspect entirely deviates from the traditional conceptions of architectural space. In the modern house, as a matter of fact, there is no longer to be found the type of architectural space, firmly enclosed and resting in itself: that product of geometric order the beauty of which consists in the balance and harmony of its proportions. Space has become mobile, its limits are melting away, its surrounding walls are blasted asunder. The rooms of the house penetrate each other and interlace in new combinations. And this not only in one plane, but simultaneously in several planes: with the partition walls between rooms, there is also eliminated the separation between the stories. The whole building from top to bottom is developed, as shown, for example, in the houses built by Le Corbusier, into a loose structure of living space. The increased opening of the outer walls, the widening of the windows, help to abolish the customary form of an optically limited space: the within is united with the without. In fact, this kind of space is no longer to be defined in terms of rigid geometry, it presents an undeterminable, indistinct, unshaped mass. In other words, space has lost its architectural autonomy. Where the structure is determined by the principle of organic order, the idea of abstract space has lost its meaning. Space becomes neutralized in its relation to architectural or style ideas, it is imagined and evaluated as cosmic space, as life-space only. And within that life-space there are planned and placed the various objects needed for the development of domestic life.

This change in the conception of space is revealed in a highly advanced example in the House Tugendhat built by Mies van der Rohe in Brno. In this house, which makes full use of the new freedom which the skeleton construction confers on the development of the ground plan, the entire domestic section of the first story is developed into a single unit, to be divided into loose parts or mere niches by screens or curtains only. Neither the unit itself nor any of its various subdivisions shows any form of optically limited space. The more so since the outer walls are entirely opened in large areas of glass, to be lowered by motor power, so that the interior becomes united with the outside world, with the all-space of the universe. Yet while the section of the first story serving the family for common use is loosened up to the extreme, the rooms of the upper story serving the private life of the single members are rather secluded. The house is located on the crest of a slope, and much as it unfolds its face to the garden and the view into the surrounding landscape, as fully it keeps its walls closed towards the street.

This house displays the new ideas in an almost programmatic form. And regarding the complete loosening of the walls in the lower floor, one might doubt whether such an interior can still afford that comfortable feeling of being sheltered which, after all, we are supposed to expect from a house. The residents, who are the first concerned with that question, felt obliged in the interest of their architect to publish their experiences (in an article in *Die Form,* the Deutscher Werkbund's magazine, in 1931). They declared that they had no reason for complaint. They ought to know, and it would be unfair to assume that the new feeling for life which finds its ease and comfort in that house, would be willing to manage without such psychical values. Only it is a different mentality in which this feeling has its roots from that of former ages, which had another idea of space and of the universe as well. In former times, space dominated

189

man, and he found his happiness in submitting himself in his own room to the autonomy of its geometric laws. In modern times, man dominates space, and consequently he also denies its limits in his own rooms.

Not alone has a changed conception of space affected the surfaces and volumes of the interior, it has also changed the character of the furniture. As long as the idea of space is autonomous, and architecture is based on geometric laws, furniture, too, becomes a bearer of the style idea. It forms an element of architectural composition, it is a means, even an integral part, of wall decoration. And as long as the furniture, besides being an object of use, is supposed to strengthen the architectural substance of the interior, it must have a formal unity, corresponding to the uniformity of style. The furniture of each single room must form what is called a set. The tendency towards style, involved in all strains of "architecture"—in contrast to "building" which knows no style—demands that a Rococo room, for instance, be furnished with a Rococo set. And so much are the single pieces of this set an integral part of the interior that its harmony would be severely impaired, its balance even entirely lost, if a single chair were removed from the place assigned to it in the whole setting. Sentenced to immobility, pinned to their places on the wall, the sofas and chairs of the Rococo period were not even covered with material on their backs.

Even the *Art Nouveau* movement, although it pleaded for the pure form of use and had also a rather clear idea of its structural problems, could not break away from the idea of style in its practical attempts to solve these problems. A room designed

PLANETARIUM, Duesseldorf, 1926. Wilhelm Kreis, architect

A light and elegant construction of concrete consisting of sixteen slender supports upholding a ring of concrete which carries the construction of the dome. The architecture—a façade of heavy masses of brick vaguely recalling Byzantine models—reveals nothing of the character and expressiveness of the technical form.

AIRDROME, Orly near Paris, 1916. E. Freyssinet, engineer

SANITARIUM, Hilversum near Amsterdam. B. Byvoet and J. Duiker, architects

by van de Velde is still under the constraint of style unity: with the furniture it also needs a tapestry and a chandelier designed by van de Velde. And so strong was the tendency in these interiors towards style unity that they were compatible, as has been proved by experience in many actual cases, with the paintings of only one school: those of the Neo-Impressionists.

In furnishing the modern house, the plan of which is no longer thought of in terms of geometrical space, there is no necessity for a fixed and formal set. Where the interior is conceived as life-space only, the furniture is freed from the imposition of style unity, and becomes again a simple object of use. Developing its proper nature, as determined by the particular demand of use, it will fulfill its purpose in every room and on every spot where it is placed. Like an oriental carpet such furniture is neutralized as to style. It will fit in every surrounding, compatible with other objects of use. It will compete even with the best masterpieces of former periods, and this the more successfully, the more strongly and purely its own individual form of use is brought out.

In the new house, furniture, instead of being part of a set, rigidly bound together by the principle of style, becomes a mobile member of an ensemble, united only by the purpose of use. This purpose may embrace characteristic pieces of all epochs, and the art of furnishing consists only in developing this mixture to a concert harmonious in form and color. The English, who always value the practical comfort of their houses more highly than their unity of style, were the first to depart from the constraint of the set. Following in their early reform of domestic building the examples shown in the indigenous dwellings of the peasantry, they came to select their furniture wherever they found it, provided that its structure and form satisfied their natural demand for comfort. This mixture of furniture of various periods, this ensemble of Queen Anne chests and Georgian side-boards, Chippendale chairs and modern lounges, gives the interior of the English house, instead of impairing its harmony, its peculiar coziness and comfort.

Now, as the minor arts live under the same laws as building, the change of structure, accomplished in house building, has also reacted upon the form of furniture. At the present time, furniture is again conceived, according to its nature, as an object of use the form of which is determined by the function it has to fulfill. And so its production aims at developing the individual character of the single object rather than at demonstrating the artistic individuality of the designer. The pure form of use is not produced by the ingenious caprice of a single artist, but it is an anonymous product, like the forms of modern technique, resulting from a process of cultivation continued through the co-operative work of generations. This process is directed towards refining the form of the object as well as enhancing its usefulness, and in the course of this process, through bettering the material, through the use of improved technique and methods of production, the form acquires visual charm and emotional values, increasing the esthetic effectiveness of the object.

It is the pure form of use, said Paul Valéry, in his Dialogue *Eupalinos, or The Architect,* that gives an impression of beauty born of exactitude, and that sort of delight engendered by the almost miraculous conformity of an object with the function that it must fulfill. "And so the perfection of this aptitude excites in our souls the feeling of a relationship between the beautiful and the necessary; and the final ease or simplicity of the result, compared with the intricacy of the problem, fills us with an indescribable enthusiasm. Unexpected elegance intoxicates us. Nothing but what is of strict utility finds a place in such happy fabrications; they no longer contain anything not solely deduced from the exigencies of the desired effect; but one feels that almost a god was needed to make so pure a deduction."

With the turn to the pure form of use modern furniture has become, in its general appearance, fundamentally simpler, but certainly not more standardized. The pure form of use is amplified by variations, and the more the demands become differentiated, the more differentiated become the forms. While all types of furniture serving for storage purposes, as for instance, closets for clothes and linens, shelves for books and the like, tend to be reduced to typical box-forms, the seating furniture is developed into highly refined modes of organic structure. As the multitude of types is unlimited, so is also the variety of forms. The series begins with the swivel chair of American descent, the earliest purely industrial product of this kind, and ends, at present, with the steel chair, which demonstrates par excellence the utilization and refinement of a new material. If the comfort of a chair demands that its shape follow the lines of the body, the steel chair has the best chance to fulfill this condition through the high elasticity of its material. Moreover, it joins the quality of perfect comfort with the decorative charm gained from the flow of its elegant lines and from the technical refinement of its material, the shining finish of nickel or chromium. But still the question remains, whether the use of steel in the making of furniture, at least for domestic purposes, is not foreign to the nature of its ultimate use, since it is always cold to the touch, and in that respect inferior to wood. The nature of its material restricts the use of steel furniture to rooms mainly devoted to sanitary purposes.

In the various types of modern seating furniture, there is perhaps best revealed the change in the style of life turning from the stiff and formal to the easy and unconventional. Whereas a Rococo chair, for instance, according to the ceremonial style to which society subjugated itself, was so built as to induce people sitting on it to pose and strike a solemn or at least restrained attitude, every type of modern seating furniture by force of its structure invites to relaxing, to stretching the limbs and lolling about. Our mode of life impresses upon the forms a particular physiognomy that distinguishes them definitely from the products of former epochs and characterizes them in their outer appearance as products of their social environment.

In the pure form of use, furniture and household objects have achieved an eternal style. Eternal are the forms of this style in contrast with the products of the "styles" characterized by the elements of their changing decoration, and therefore of temporary validity. But precisely in these eternal forms the modern objects have achieved conformity with the age. Freed from the confection of applied ornament, showing the object again in its original shape, the pure form of use is neutralized not only as

194

TUGENDHAT HOUSE, Brno, Czechoslovakia, 1930. Garden façade and interior. Mies van der Rohe, architect

(Courtesy Department of Architecture, Museum of Modern Art, New York)

HOUSING DEVELOPMENT,
Holland, 1927. J. J. P. Oud,
architect

to time and style but also as to differences of social rank. In the pure form of use, the objects are freed from the implication of being an index of social status. Look at clothing, for example: in the change of social structure we have abandoned particular costumes representing different ranks. The banker's secretary wears an evening gown of quite the same pattern as his wife, except that hers is of silk, while that of the secretary is only of rayon. The banker's wife wears with her evening gown a necklace of pearls, and so does his secretary, though hers is of Tecla pearls (and frequently that of the banker's wife, too, because the genuine ones are kept in the bank vault for safety). And so as to furniture, it has practically become uniform for the various classes differing only in quality of material and execution.

Such sociological facts account for the approval of the pure form of use characteristic of the taste of the age. This approval manifests itself in our decided admiration for the forms produced by modern technique; it is reflected in the entire outward appearance of both sexes, through the innumerable fluctuations of fashion particularly in dress, with its tendency to conform in pattern to the natural movements of the body.

And it is not only an esthetic value which in our days is attributed to the pure form of use; it is also a cultural and even ethical value. For, in a time when all traditional forms of life are breaking asunder, and new ones have not arisen as yet, only the very elementary and very simple can be felt and valued as the very true and genuine. In the pure form of use, all structure appears again in its basic form, the form of eternal validity, and therefore, for us, the only one which is true.

4. HOUSING: A COLLECTIVE NECESSITY

THE NEED OF A NEW TYPE

Nothing perhaps shows better how much the development of new types depends upon the sociological conditions of the time than the situation in housing. Nowhere are more clearly to be seen the retarding and promoting influences exercised by time itself, the dependence of fruition on the ripeness of time, than in the calamitous fate of attempts to solve this important problem. Since the beginning of the Industrial Revolution, since the craftsman departed from his native soil and migrated to the large cities, since his work became industrial labor, the housing problem has been acute, urgently demanding a solution. The problem, shortly defined, consists in providing a type of dwelling appropriate to the particular needs and requirements of that new social stratum which was to form the broad basis of the new industrial structure. The requisite type would have been a small dwelling, consisting of about three or four rooms, according to the income level of that class, and at the so-called reasonable rent, a monthly rent not higher than one week's wages.

The development of the new type needed for that new social stratum, which at present, according to statistics, forms about 80 to 90 per cent of the urban population, including not only the working classes but also large parts of the white-collar middle classes, was left, in accordance with the principles of contemporary economics, to the free interplay of economic forces. The results are known.

Housing became a mere branch of real estate business, which concerned itself with the realization of growing land values rather than with the real needs of the community. The small dwelling, not realized at all as a special type, needing a special development and a particular method of land division, was at first evolved on the remnants left over from the development of the high class dwelling, and these remnants were considered good enough, for people condemned to use them, for human habitation.

In New York, for instance, when with the rise of the business district at the tip of Manhattan the well-to-do left their three story houses to move uptown, these houses were altered into multi-family houses by adding a wing at the back, covering almost the whole area of the former garden; and this slipshod method of procedure, not hindered by any building restrictions, was finally established as a norm with the development of the old and new tenement house. The dwellings of the working population became masses of frightful congestion.

In Berlin, the example of which was followed in great parts of Germany, the rent-barracks system grew out of a disastrous town planning scheme providing uniform blocks of large depth, and the cheap dwelling became literally a by-product of the high class apartment facing the street: a poor cramped cheerless flat in a back building, five or six stories high, opening upon a narrow yard, without air or light and getting no sun at all.

And so it was all over the industrialized world; the one exception was in England where common sense and a highly developed feeling for social responsibility and domestic life established the small one-family house as the normal type for working class dwellings.

Society's improvident treatment of the housing problem fostered the very seeds of its own retribution. The reaction was devastating in every sense, socially, economically, and politically. The great damage done to public health was revealed in the frightful figures on tuberculosis and infant mortality. Moreover, with the need of subletting rooms to boarders, enforced by the pressure of high rents, these scanty dwellings turned into breeding places of vice and crime and juvenile delinquency. There is a definite relationship between the social environment and the social product, and "where both sexes and all ages are herded together without possibilities of day and night separation, there it is difficult, if not impossible, to keep up certain standards of morals." And housing conditions also react upon the sense of citizenship, upon the attitude of the citizen toward society and state. It is, indeed, the overpopulated slum district that sends out the public enemy, the man who can never adapt himself to a society tolerating the unworthy conditions he comes from. With good reason, the growing estrangement of the working classes, observed in Germany in pre-war times, was attributed by leading politicians to the inadequate housing conditions, generating among the masses a feeling of having no roots at all. And if the social crisis spreading all over the world has not yet

ROEMER HOUSE, Altona-Oth-
marschen, Germany, 1927-1928.
Karl Schneider, architect

BUCHROITHNER HOUSE,
Zell-am-See, 1928. Leo Welzen-
bacher, architect

MICHAELSEN HOUSE, and view from interior. Altona-Blankenese, Germany, 1923. Karl Schneider, architect

gripped England, and her social structure still remains fairly intact, one wonders whether it is not to some extent because of her wise and far-sighted housing policy.

The methods of housing production, followed by private enterprise for more than a century, have proved unsatisfactory. And no hope for improvement is left because they are wrong at the roots. These methods are based on a scheme dividing the single block into small individual lots which in their size and form were adequate as long as they were built upon with single private houses. But when such lots were used for multi-family houses they simply enforced the overcoverage of land with building. The problem of the architect in designing his plans was, then, confined to figuring out by tricky methods of calculation the highest possible coverage of land, in order to realize its high speculative values. And to quote from the Regional Survey of New York and Its Environs, "as long as it is more important to maintain the interests of those who benefit from high land values and congested areas than the general prosperity of the country," no progress in solving the housing problem is obtainable. Every attempt, even of the most talented architect, to improve or embellish the product derived from such a method, was condemned to be futile, and even the best architecture could not disguise the social problems hidden behind the ostentatious façades.

There was even in pre-war times a full understanding of the situation, so devastating to public health and morals. Housing experts in all countries had realized the defects of the traditional methods of production, and showed the way needed for their removal. Moreover, these proposals had proved their practical value and usefulness with the numerous experiments carried through by co-operative housing societies. Their work showed in practice that even when high land values necessitated the building of multi-family houses, much better results could be obtained by replacing the obsolete subdivision of the block into small single lots by large scale construction, with the whole area of the block as building unit.

Their excellent demonstrations of the possible development of the small dwelling into a type of its own remained isolated; the studies and practical proposals of the experts were not generally followed. For, to make them ready for realization, certain deviations were necessary from the principles of the existing economic system, and new legal statutes and institutions had to be established. As these changes, however, interfered with the traditional conceptions of capitalistic economy and with the privileged power of private interests, they were bound to fail.

Here it becomes manifest that the housing problem is not a technical or building problem only, but also, and in a predominant sense, an economic and political problem. Here it becomes clear that a unified state of society is the main prerequisite for the rise and development of new building types. It needed, in fact, the energizing repercussions of a war to make the times ripe for those changes demanded by the experts, and to provide the sociological background for their execution.

The crisis of thought following the World War brought about a new social concept bringing home to public opinion the idea of social responsibility, of social control and readjustment.

With this change of public opinion it became possible, at least in the field of housing, to deviate from the principles of private economy and to enact such restrictions and amendments of public law as were needed for social housing. Moreover, with the political revolutions following the war in such countries as Germany, Austria, and Russia, the influence of the working class was strengthened to such a degree that they could finally realize their just claims, so long entirely neglected, to a dwelling type of their own.

The consequences of the World War radically changed the housing situation in virtually all European countries as well as in the United States. This situation was characterized by a growing housing shortage, caused by the complete stagnation of private building in the belligerent countries. This stagnation, keeping on in the first years after the war because of the lack of building credits, was followed by a general decline of speculative land values. This historical moment was used in such countries as Germany and Austria to establish a new housing policy. As under the prevailing circumstances private enterprise, working for profit, was not able to provide housing on an ordinary commercial basis, housing was declared a public utility, in the same sense as education, water supply, fire and police protection. As building credits had to be furnished for the most part from public sources, they were entrusted to co-operative building societies and limited dividend companies, at any rate to organizations working on a non-commercial basis. Thereby housing production was freed from the disastrous dependency on land speculation, and finally the builder and contractor was made again what he ought to be: the chief organizer of the process of production. And as a public utility, housing was brought almost entirely under public control, embracing not only rental scales, but the whole development of housing schemes, including location, planning, building methods, dwelling type and equipment.

Working under conditions so favorably changed, the architect was faced with a task extremely stimulating to his creative instinct, his craft and skill. Freed from the degrading job of being a handy man of the realtor working only for the great game of land exploitation, he found his way open to devote all his talents exclusively to the practical, technical and architectural problems of housing. Now, for the first time, it became his task to develop, in accordance with actual and clearly defined needs, and with all the aid of technical science, a new type of small dwelling.

His work started with the development of new methods of layout. The obsolete scheme of subdividing the block in individual plots, characteristic of the old tenement house system, was entirely abandoned, and replaced by a system adapted to the principles of large scale construction, connecting in one homogeneous plan the area not only of a single block, but of entire city districts. With the whole block as a unit, only its borders are built upon, and with the structures no more than two rooms deep. Rear buildings and courtyards are thereby eliminated, and replaced by large open spaces in the interior of the block, developed into common gardens and playgrounds for children. Constant attempts to lower both the cost of layout and the proportion of land coverage finally led to the "strip building method" (Zeilenbau). With this method, up to now the last stage of development, the blocks are arranged on the area to be built upon in long parallel rows, oriented according to the needs of latitude and climate, but irrespective of the direction of the main traffic and communicating roads. For direct access to the single houses, small paths are provided and narrow sidewalks, lightly paved, to be used only for pedestrians. This new method, only possible under the new freedom procured by large scale operation, also secures the utmost economy in street building. Moreover, it does completely away with all sorts of courts, entirely abolishing the differentiation of front and rear. Both façades are now of equal value as to their architectural aspect as well as for dwelling purposes, and every single dwelling unit in such a super-block enjoys the same advantage of exposure to the sun.

With this new method of layout, there appears a new concept of town planning; a concept revealing the structural ideas of organic order with its attempt to restore to the city the natural world of the open landscape. With this concept, however, are also abandoned the esthetic ideas of town planning, inherited from Renaissance and Baroque times. The street, now regarded according to its natural function as a mere organ of traffic, is freed from the esthetic function of representing the idea of architectural space. And the blocks, no longer supposed to form with their façades the enclosing walls of this architectural space, are simply placed within the open space of the urban scene, and grouped according to the demands of exposure and the needs of light and air.

The second and no less important task for the architect was the development of the new types of small dwellings, appropriate in their plans to the living standards and the social concepts of the prospective occupants. As with these standards narrow limits are assigned to the extent of dwelling space, it becomes the more important to provide the best and most economical use of the habitable floor area. Methodical studies have been made for the planning of rooms in regard to domestic arrangement, especially to kitchen arrangement, in order to simplify housekeeping and to lighten the work of housewives. By way of numerous experiments, an exact scientific method of planning has been developed, demonstrating how to construct in every detail the single dwelling cell. It is the basic idea of that method that the dwelling unit is a tool of living which in its form and structure has to be adapted to the manifold functions of domestic life, such as working and resting, cooking and eating. And it is the guiding principle of this method that the particular function each single room has to serve determines its size and shape, the distribution of the windows and doors and even the arrangement of the furniture.

In developing the new types, it has become an almost general practice to make the living-room as large as possible and to restrict the other rooms to the smallest size compatible with the dimensions of the necessary furniture. In most of the new housing developments, the furniture is built-in, wherever possible, sometimes even the beds, not only to save space but also to avoid cluttering with superfluous movables which impede cleaning. And the kitchen, equipped with all sorts of built-in furniture—

wall cupboards, working tables, range, sink and tap—so arranged as to afford the highest degree of work economy, has developed into a sort of laboratory, its floor space reduced to a minimum. The limitation of habitable area, characteristic of these small housing schemes, is offset by freeing the single unit from former demands on floor space through the transfer of private domestic functions to new commercial units, such as central heating plants, central baths and laundries, common garden courts, nurseries, and playgrounds for children.

The new multi-family house resulting from this development, a building limited to three stories with two apartments on one landing and therefore avoiding the former congestion, has nothing in common with the old tenement except the name. In this new type of multi-family house the small dwelling unit changed from the monstrosity it had been in the former mass-tenement to a well-shaped organic unit, to a living cell, full of life and friendly to life, a cell from which a healthy and well-formed city structure could be developed. While in former days the disorder of small single façades made impossible a homogeneous architectural effect even within one single street, the new method of housing production, based on large-scale operation, develops great districts of the urban area into harmonious neighborhood units provided with the amenities of a human environment. The houses, always recurring in uniform types and arranged in long rows, are united under a common roof. These large groups, forming the architectural units of the housing scheme, are varied by different groupings of the building masses.

As their main and characteristic feature, however, uniformity prevails in these new housing schemes, as in the demands of the occupants, so in their architectural aspect. Their occupants are more or less of the same income group, and their living standards do not allow much scope for individual preferences. This sociological fact finds its obvious expression in the architectural physiognomy of these new housing developments. Their architectural uniformity is compulsory since it is inherent in the conditions of the project. For the same reason, the former romantic tendency to imagine the suburb as a sort of village has been abandoned—the tendency still followed by the more conservative architects in England who develop their plans as a network of winding streets, sometimes arbitrarily curved, and use the half-rural cottage type with its picturesque pitched roofs and gables. The modern architect, however, conceives his project as a definite sub-*urban* scheme, as a separate residential section for a specific town-folk, for a population that works in the city, but after work wants to live in an environment offering the advantages of outdoor recreation and close contact with nature.

The results of this new building activity imbued with a new social spirit are amazing in both quantity and quality. Take Germany, for example; up to the war, she was one of the most backward nations in the field of housing, and the country which attracted the eyes of the whole world by its model social legislation had to put up with the doubtful reputation of being the country of the rent-barrack. Since the war her backwardness has been more than made up, and indeed changed into an almost advanced position, if one is permitted to draw conclusions from the eagerness of foreign experts to study German housing

HOUSING DEVELOPMENT, Zehlendorf near Berlin. Bruno Taut, architect

OLD PEOPLE'S HOME, Frankfort, Germany, 1929. Mart Stam, architect

SILO, Kvarholmen near Stockholm, 1927. S. Wallander, architect

SCHOOL, Suresnes, France. Beaudion and Lods, architects

and from their cordial expressions of approval. "In Germany," said Catherine Bauer in her book on Modern Housing, "the period after the War up to 1931 marks the most fruitful epoch of modern housing which the World has yet to show." Many a German town undertook large housing programs well related to a carefully prepared extension plan for the city.

In Berlin, for instance, the native town of the rent-barracks, the odious type of mass tenement was entirely stamped out, and with the new housing schemes, developed in the outskirts and environs of the city, the way has been opened to a systematic decentralization, relieving the congested districts of the inner city. The new developments, some of them containing more than 5000 dwellings, are distributed all around the fringes of the city, in accordance with the needs of the population and with regard to the existing public services and means of communication. The spacious housing schemes built everywhere in the outskirts make a pleasant transition from the densely covered areas of the city to the open landscape. Each of these developments is based on a homogeneous plan, but divided into various groups, and each group is designed by a different architect, a method providing variety in their architectural appearance in spite of the uniformity of the types.

The city of Frankfort, under the direction of the City Architect, Ernst May, developed within its program of 25,000 houses a number of new suburbs, located in the spectacular landscape of the Nidda Valley and framed by the hills of the Taunus Mountains. To the uniformity of their houses the vegetation, the trees and the green of the gardens brings an enlivening element. And after all, the reduced coverage and the low density of building obtained in all these new schemes affords to their inhabitants a cheering sense of spaciousness, assuring even in the narrow limits of a minimum dwelling ration a healthy existence worthy of human beings.

In the European countries, in the years after the war, housing became the favorite experimental field of those progressive forces that proclaimed the new spirit of building. In the new housing projects the principles of modern building have been tested, approved, and carried out. Moreover, in such countries as Germany, Austria and Switzerland housing has been made the object of special exhibitions, providing an opportunity for advanced experiments. On these occasions, many a project has been carried through, as audacious in its design as provocative in its new forms, anticipating within the society as it is the conception of a new social order and the demands of a society to come.

5. A NEW CITY TYPE

Last, let us look at that proper and most original product of the era of capitalism: the modern city, that new center of national economy quite unparalleled as to its origin, size, and administrative problems in history.

The Industrial Revolution came upon the cities like a thief in the night, said Patrick Geddes. The cities, entirely unprepared for the implied moral and economic changes, grew simply by accretion; things were left to the free interplay of economic forces, and there was no thought for tomorrow, no foresight, no planning for the wise use of land. The new industrial plants were placed by chance and scattered over the urban area, overhanging the whole city with the dust of their smoke stacks, ruining the water front and devastating the natural environment, the recreation ground of the urban population. An intricate network of railroads and freight yards was spread over the urban area, blocking the flow of interurban traffic and causing a harmful friction of space which prevented a sound and efficient development of the city as a whole. In many a city, particularly in mining towns, industrial areas, transportation lines and residential sections overlapped, hindering each other in their efficiency. Blind railway tracks blocked the extension of industrial plants, and inversely, the industrial plants hindered the building of the necessary streets and the extension of railroad lines. On the other hand, residential sections were established on ground which in turn hindered the extension of mines and means of transportation, so that they had to be torn down before they were obsolete from use.

In short, the city, left to the interplay of so many different and heterogeneous interests, became a sheer agglomeration of random building, and developed into a rank weed, disclosing all the symptoms of disastrous hypertrophy. And even the outer appearance of its monumental civic center, of its pompous avenues and luxurious plazas, displaying the growing wealth of the community, could by no means compensate for the social misery revealed in the dreary slum districts and the overcrowded tenements falling far below any decent standard of human habitation.

THE CITY AS AN INTEGRATED ORGANISM

After a century of such haphazard growth, the city has now entered a new stage of its development, carefully prepared by a plan, a plan reflecting in its concept the ideas of organic structure. During the nineteenth century, the city was conceived as a purely mechanical structure consisting of an aggregation of technical elements, such as streets and blocks, gas and water pipes, railroads and highways: elements, however, more disintegrated than co-ordinated, and often disturbing and even upsetting each other by friction of space. Under the influence of the new spirit of building this mechanical concept has been abandoned, and the city is now thought of as a living organism the growth of

HOUSING DEVELOPMENT, Berlin. Paul Mebes, architect

FLATS AT HIGHPOINT, London, 1933. Tecton Group, architects
(*Courtesy The Architectural Review, London*)

UNITY HOUSE, Bushkill, Pa.
Dining Hall. William Lescaze,
architect

PHILADELPHIA SAVINGS
FUND SOCIETY, Bank and Office Building. Howe and Lescaze, architects

UNITY HOUSE. Outdoor Pavilion. William Lescaze, architect

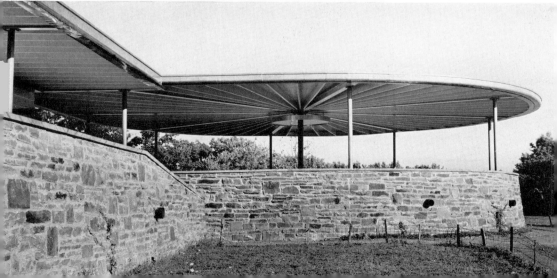

which is guided by a general plan: a plan not dealing with local developments or detailed subdivision of land, but presenting a general program for the future development of the city, an imaginative picture, so to speak, demonstrating how the city should grow and extend in the future. An imaginative picture, but nevertheless strictly based on reality, on the immutable facts by which the city is bounded in its organic growth—the physical, economic and social conditions of its existence. These facts, assembled by the geographer, the economist and the sociologist and laid down in the civic survey describing the nature, the character and the function of the city organism, form the solid base for the city planner's work. This work, however, is solely directed towards preparing for the organic growth of the city by providing for the wise and economic use of the urban land.

Taking the city as a living organism, it has to be developed into a structure serving its various functions with the highest degree of efficiency. The city is a rather complicated organism, serving first for work, in its manifold ramifications, including the various activities of trade, commerce and industry, next, for communication, and finally for housing and recreation. And as a living organism, the city practices these vital functions in permanent mutual interaction. Thus, the general plan, adjusting these various functions to special organs, divides the urban area in different zones, such as transportation zones, business quarters— including both commercial and industrial zones—residential quarters and green zones. Providing in advance certain areas of the urban ground for the purposes they are best suited to, according to their location or physical features, the plan prepares the proper and economic utilization of the urban land. And the art of planning consists in arranging and distributing these various areas all over the urban ground in accordance with the requirements of their inner dynamics and functional relationship, thus eliminating for the future any friction of space.

In the modern city, according to such an organic plan, the main business districts, the seats of trade and commerce, the banks and office buildings, are concentrated in the central areas, closely connected with the main railway stations. The industrial plants, however, the factories, workshops, and storehouses, are not concentrated in one area alone in order to avoid traffic congestion and overcrowding in the residential sections of the working population. Industrial zones, differentiated for light and heavy industries, are distributed throughout the city. To further systematic decentralization large areas are provided for heavy industries on the fringes of the city, in close connection with the main freight yards, with waterways, canals, and commercial harbors. Near to these industrial districts new housing schemes are developed to shorten the daily travel between home and working place. And these residential sections are separated from the industrial districts, and protected against the fatal nuisance of their dust and smoke by large green zones, by parks and playgrounds. Developed into a continuous system spreading all over the urban territory and involving any area of natural vegetation, any water planes, brooks, and lakes, these green zones penetrate the whole city, breaking as far as possible even into the inner districts, into the core of the city and loosening the density of building. And even the transportation zones provided in the general plan for needs to come, for enlargements or new construction of all sorts of communication ways, railroads, highways, waterways, airports and so forth, should be used, as long as they are not needed, for open space and park grounds.

A NEW CITY TYPE IN THE MAKING

With the realization of these new ideas of planning, based on the orderly differentiation and interrelation of both functions and structures, a new city type begins to arise. The modern city, instead of sprawling itself in an uncontrolled growth that would relentlessly engulf the countryside of field and forest, proceeds by planned settlements, by garden suburbs and satellite towns, growing gradually into its natural surroundings. Interpreting this new tendency towards decentralization, one may suppose that the sharp boundaries between urban and rural districts, which we took as a given fact up to now, will loosen up in the future. It seems as though we were entering a new epoch in the history of human settlement. In the Middle Ages, agricultural and industrial activities became definitely separated, and the town became sharply distinguished from the surrounding rural district, its boundaries marked by walls characterizing the urban community as an independent seat of economy and administration. It seems that in our time this principal distinction between town and country will be more and more wiped out, that the modern city, following the fundamental changes of economic structure and according to the new conditions and needs of social life, bursts its boundaries, wandering out again into the country. It seems that town and country begin to penetrate

213

each other, fusing the two ways of life, thereby restoring to man a natural and healthful life of work and play.

FROM TOWN PLANNING TO REGIONAL PLANNING

Therefore, the timely provision for the wise use of land must not stop at the borderline of the urban territory itself. The urban development can no longer be considered as a problem by itself, but must be treated in a larger connection, as a part of the general problem of human settlement. In fact, town planning has been supplemented in our time by another and wider planning activity; and if anything can prove the new mode of thinking characteristic of our time, which conceives the problem of structure in terms of organic order, then it is that fresh and most promising branch on the tree of the Arts which is called Regional Planning.

The regional concept, directed towards developing an area into an organic unity, has supplanted the traditional concept of political boundaries which usually arise by pure chance, the historical heritage of previous wars or conquest. This static concept of the political territory has been replaced by the dynamic concept of the geographical region the unit of which is to be determined by the laws of its growth set by the physical conditions of the area and its economic functions and its social needs. Defining the region as "an area where land-work-folk fuse into a pattern coherent within, but differentiated from other regions without," regional planning deals with the development of cities and countrysides, of industrial and natural resources, as parts of a regional whole. And by organizing the area according to the requirements of its social, economic and cultural life and its relationship to other regions, regional planning aims at developing the region into an organism so well adapted to its environment that it can fulfill, with the highest degree of efficiency, all the various functions it has to serve for the good life of man.

In European countries, the need for regional planning was first felt in territories where abundant raw materials had called forth a conglomeration of industry, and therewith a fatal congestion of population. In England, the large coal districts in Kent and Wales, in Germany the rich mining region on the Ruhr, form a continuous area of cities, interlacing in each other and almost melting together. This development, for which Patrick Geddes, in his book *Cities in Evolution* coined the new term of "conurbation," caused an acute state of congestion, local friction and waste, whose difficult problems could be overcome only by a wider concept of planning, surpassing the municipal limits and establishing a new administrative area taking within its boundaries "all that was really functional for the whole region." Meanwhile, the regional concept has been generally adopted for reconstruction such overdeveloped areas as are exemplified by most metropolitan regions. And in the United States the Tennessee Valley project, now under construction, represents an experiment demonstrating the potentialities of regional planning for the problem of an underdeveloped region; a region, however, which in its natural conditions and economic possibilities affords all prerequisites for a new standard of civilization to be established.

A NEW OUTLOOK

With the turn to the ideas of organic order, we are advancing in planning from smaller to ever-larger units. From the former layout of single lots for individual houses, we advanced to the larger unit of the neighborhood. When the larger population centers spread their influence over the surrounding areas, we extended the field of planning from the city to the larger unit of the metropolitan region. Realizing the relationship of the metropolitan region to the larger unit of the geographical region of which it is a part, we advanced to regional planning, taking in not only the urban centers but the groups of cities, and of highways, and of natural resources that make up a unified district. In developing the regional concept, however, we discovered that there is also an interrelationship between these regions, and we are now advancing to state, and even to national planning, preparing a new organization of the national territory by dividing its area into regions of organic unity.

This progress in planning toward larger and larger units opens a new and hopeful outlook for the future. In the long run, the new concept of planning, guided by the principles of organic order, will not be restricted to that largest unit we have reached up to now, that unit which is determined by the political boundaries of a nation. In our dynamic life, there is going on a continuous interaction between the various nations and countries all over the world. This interaction will and must lead to a new plan of the world, in which the outworn ideas of inflexible political boundaries will give way to a new dynamic and flexible organic order, setting up a new entity of component and interrelated parts, which in closest association and peaceful co-operation render effective service to the welfare of the greater Commonwealth.

SUMMARY: THE FUTURE
OF MODERN BUILDING

The new spirit of building, and the movement which it has originated, is of an international character, as is the crisis of order from which it is derived. The problem pursued in the new spirit is common to all nations, rising from the same needs and inducing spiritual alliances that cross national boundaries for its solution.

It is for this reason that the works of modern building show a striking conformity all over the world, an almost style-like similarity of their form. Indeed, the works of modern building still largely lack the differentiating note of national touch and character. The same happened at the rise of the Gothic: its modernism, too, grew out of the ground of a common building problem—the construction of the ribbed vault—which finally was brought to its solution in a spiritual alliance of the Western nations. And it was only in the historical course of its development that the style gained its differentiating features derived from the various and diversifying influences of national traditions and local peculiarities.

With the national coloring, the forms of modern building also lack, as yet, that individual touch resulting from the refining hands of the single master. But as long as the general solution of a problem is to be found, involving the development of a new type, the work of the single individuality becomes merged in the co-operative work of the group. This turn from emphasizing the individual talent to devoting it to the common problem is also a characteristic noted in all times of important transformations in art. It is necessary first of all, said Wilhelm Pinder, to set up something new, a whole to which the work of the following generations will then bring the differentiating features.

The creation of this new general form which the times call for—that is the present aim of the new spirit of building. It is the *Zeitgeist,* the spirit of the age, which incarnates its form in modern building. As to the esthetic quality of this form, it cannot be denied that it still suffers from the tendency towards modernism, as form always does from any kind of tendency. In its present state, there is very little to be said as to its artistic substance. As yet this form can be spoken of and evaluated only by considering the mental attitude from which it originated. The form of modern building may still be crude, sober, and unfinished, resembling in this tentative nature the unsettled age in which it arises. But it also reveals new mental content, it manifests a new value-concept related to the ideal of a new society that is now emerging.

This brings us back to our starting point. Building, as a function of the community, is a social art. It is from society that the architect gets his task, and it is society that gives him the stuff that he has to mold into form. To the architect, society is both abettor and mediator of his creative work, which would be an effort *in vacuo* if dependent on itself. Thus, among the decisive factors the work of the architect is bounded by, the social conditions under which he enters his task, are of the greatest importance—a fact which led Jakob Burckhardt to the conclusion that greatness in architecture is more a product of the time in question than of one or the other great master.

Greatness, however, is denied in our time not only to architecture, but apparently to all art. In this era of social transformation, life centers around other problems than those of art and artistic imagination. In the new spirit, however, in which this time tries to overcome those other problems arising from the crisis of order, there are also rooted the principal ideas that guide the international movement of new building. As a driving force by its moral principles, as a formative power in the sociological field, the movement has proved its rejuvenating and enlivening strength. And, therefore, the future belongs to it. Yet while it is true that the spirit of new building can only grow and thrive in an atmosphere where the driving forces of this time are felt and affirmed, it is likewise true that its forms can only unfold and ripen to full maturity in the same measure as the changing ideas of order succeed in accomplishing a new form of society.

NOTES

INTRODUCTION:

4, 15   quotation see Bibl. Nr. 3, vol. I, p. 104.

5, 17   two elemental impulses that grow out of a common root see: Bibl. Nr. 11. Gundolf explains the struggle between classicism and romanticism as derived from two antagonistic impulses of the creative instinct. He also distinguishes between "intuitive and constructive forces." l. c., p. 322.

6, 27   polarity of creative impulse
cf. Wilhelm Pinder, *Das Problem der Generation;* Berlin, 1926, p. 141.

10, 2   quoted from F. Haverfield, cf. Bibl. Nr. 13, p. 14. As to the dualism of form in city planning cf. Bibl. Nr. 8.

13, 21   Bibl. Nr. 4, p. 131.

15, 4   see Alfred N. Whitehead, *Science and the Modern World;* New York, The Macmillan Co. 1926. p. 150.

Part One: CHAPTER 1:

21, 13   The Renaissance, seen from a sociological point of view: quotation taken from Ernst Troeltsch: *Aufsätze zur Geistesgeschichte und Religionssoziologie.* Ges. Schriften, vol. iv, p. 759.

21, 20   Bibl. Nr. 6, p. 258.

35, 22   The attitude of this school is clearly expressed by Ralph Adams Cram: "What we confront today is the chaos of change when one era comes to its end and another rises to take its place. This being so, the architect or other artist . . . is and must be an eclectic—an opportunist, if you like. The new must be expressed through new, but perfectly well-chosen words; the old, which still providentially survives, through its old language, adapted and made intelligible to the modern consciousness; the future—if, by the grace of God, some may be granted an adumbration of its nature—in that idiom that preserves and indicates eternal values supplemented and enriched by that which is good (and that alone) which develops from the peculiar processes of the present time." cf. *My Life in Architecture*. Boston, Little, Brown & Co., 1936, p. 279.

CHAPTER 2:

39, 4 and 24 Schinkel's diary. Bibl. Nr. 31, p. 194.

45, 28 *Stimmungs-Realismus,* cf. Oscar Gehrig, *Friedrich Georg Kersting;* Rostock, Mecklenburgische Gesellschaft, 1932.

47, 14 James Bogardus and the cast iron front. cf. Lewis Mumford, Bibl. Nr. 26, p. 111.

47, 28 competition for the invention of a new style: cf. Bibl. Nr. 12. p. 453.

CHAPTER 3:

51, 28 quotation from W. R. Lethaby, cf. Bibl. Nr. 21. p. 19.

52, 6 as to Morris's social philosophy, cf. the excellent study of Anna A. von Helmholtz-Phelan, Bibl. Nr. 14.

54, 27 Bibl. Nr. 22.

58, 1 examples of Morris's pattern designing: see Bibl. Nrs. 7 and 37.

65, 1 Norman Shaw and the problem of the small house: see Bibl. Nr. 28, vol. i, p. 101.

Part Two: CHAPTER 2:

77, 16 Protest of the artist against the Eiffel Tower: cf. Bibl. Nr. 30, p. 36.

78, 8 Van de Velde's definition of the engineers as a new class of artists: see Bibl. Nr. 38, p. 111.

88, 24 see Gotthard Jedlicka: *Toulouse-Lautrec.* Berlin, Bruno Cassirer, 1928.

91, 11 cf. Henry van de Velde, l. c. p. 91.

93, 6 a recent study on Ledoux: see Bibl. Nr. 16.

96, 4 Adolf Loos' work: see Bibl. Nr. 17.

99, 24 The bold effect of these simple structures was felt by American architects, too. Among the things H. H. Richardson wanted most to design, he mentioned "a grain-elevator and the interior of a great steamboat." cf. Bibl. Nr. 39, p. 22.

CHAPTER 3:

110, 21   Richardson's railroad stations: cf. Bibl. Nr. 39, p. 100.

114, 9   About the two events in Sullivan's formative years see Bibl. Nr. 34.

116, 19   For Greenough's ideas and his definition of the principle of structure see particularly the articles, "Relative and Independent Beauty" and "Structure and Organization," Bibl. Nr. 36, pp. 131 and 170.

117, 1   The letter Greenough wrote to Emerson quoted from Van Wyck Brook, *The Flowering of New England*. p. 453.

117, 11   Sullivan the founder of a new philosophy of building, see H. Morrison, Bibl. Nr. 25, p. 229.

123, 24   One of the members of the commission: Augustus Saint-Gaudens, see Bibl. Nr. 24, vol. i, p. 47.

124, 27   Charles Eliot Norton's characterization of the Chicago Exposition: quoted from Ch. Moore Bibl. Nr. 24, vol. i, p. 87.

133, 3   H. de Fries in his study on *Frank Lloyd Wright,* Berlin, E. Pollack, 1926.

138, 9   Burckhardt's statement see Bibl. Nr. 5, p. 119.

139, 1   see Wright's autobiography Bibl. Nr. 42, p. 164.

139, 12   the first monograph on Wright's work published in Germany in 1911: see Bibl. Nr. 1.

Part Three: CHAPTER 1:

149, 15   Cubism in architecture: see J. J. P. Oud's article on "The Influence of Frank Lloyd Wright on the Architecture in Europe" in H. T. Wijdeveld, *The Life-work of the American Architect Frank Lloyd Wright*. Bibl. Nr. 40, p. 88.

151, 6   Medieval sculpture of about 1400: see Wilhelm Pinder: *Die Deutsche Plastik vom ausgehenden Mittelalter bis zum Ende der Renaissance*. Potsdam, 1924. Erster Teil, p. 39.

161, 18   "Trois Rappels," cf. Bibl. Nr. 18, p. 21.

164, 9   Corbusier's studies on the problem of the metropolis: cf. Bibl. Nr. 19.

CHAPTER 2:

172, 1   expressionism in architecture: see Walter Strich's essay, "Bemerkungen zum Begriff des Expressionismus in der Architektur" in *Die Dioskuren,* Jahrbuch für Geisteswissenschaften. Zweiter Band, 1923.

181, 18   the spirit of the age not longing for the monumental: see Schinkel Bibl. Nr. 32, vol. iii, p. 371.

184, 18   tendency towards reducing the living space: "Nearly everyone is now satisfied with less floor space than used to be demanded in former times. . . . In New York, the average size of apartments has dropped since the war. From 4.15 rooms in 1912 it had fallen to 3.34 in 1928. During the same period there was a remarkable increase in the number of three-room apartments, of which 5,346 were built in 1912 and 39,849 in 1928. The number of two-room apartments built went up about seven times, that of one-room apartments increased about 50 per cent, that of five-room apartments fell off about one-third." cf. R. L. Duffus: *Mastering a Metropolis;* New York, 1930, p. 96.

192, 25   quotation taken from Paul Valéry, *Eupalinos, or the Architect.* Translated by William McCausland Stewart. London, H. Milford, Oxford University Press, 1932. p. 74.

CHAPTER 4:
198, 16   quotation see Bibl. Nr. 43, p. 6.

CHAPTER 5:
214, 24   Definition of the region according to T. J. Woofter, Jr.: The Tennessee Basin. *The American Journal of Sociology,* vol. xxxix, July 1933—May 1934, p. 809.

BIBLIOGRAPHY

A. Books used or quoted:

1. Ashbee, Charles Robert: *Frank Lloyd Wright;* Ausgeführte Bauten, Berlin, E. Wasmuth, 1911.

2. Bauer, Catherine: *Modern Housing;* Boston and New York, Houghton Mifflin Co., 1934.

3. Bielschowsky, Albert: *The Life of Goethe;* New York and London, G. P. Putnam's Sons, 1907-09, 3 vols.

4. Branford, Victor, and Geddes, Patrick: *The Coming Polity;* London, Williams and Norgate, 1917.

5. Burckhardt, Jakob: *Geschichte der Renaissance in Italien,* Vierte Auflage. Bearbeitet von Dr. Heinrich Holtzinger; Stuttgart, Paul Neff, 1904.

6. —— *Der Cicerone;* Neunte Auflage, Leipzig, E. A. Seemann, 1904.

7. Crow, Gerald H.: *William Morris, Designer,* the Special Winter Number of the Studio, London, 1934.

8. Gantner, Joseph: *Grundformen der Europäischen Stadt;* Vienna, Anton Schroll, 1928.

9. Geddes, Patrick: *Cities in Evolution;* London, Williams and Norgate, 1915.

10. Grimme, Karl Maria: *Peter Behrens und seine Wiener akademische Meisterschule;* Vienna, Adolf Luser, 1930.

11. Gundolf, Friedrich: *Shakespeare und der Deutsche Geist;* Berlin, Georg Bondi, 1923.

12. Gurlitt, Cornelius: *Die deutsche Kunst des Neunzehnten Jahrhunderts;* Berlin, Georg Bondi, 1910.

13. Haverfield, F.: *Ancient Town-Planning;* Oxford, Clarendon Press, 1913.

14. Helmholtz-Phelan, Anna A. von: *The Social Philosophy of William Morris;* Durham, N. C., Duke University Press, 1927.

227

BIBLIOGRAPHY

15. Hitchcock, Henry-Russell, Jr.: *The Architecture of H. H. Richardson and His Times;* New York, Museum of Modern Art, 1936.

16. Kaufmann, Emil: *Von Ledoux bis Le Corbusier;* Vienna, Dr. Rolf Passer, 1933.

17. Kulka, Heinrich: *Adolf Loos;* Vienna, Anton Schroll, 1931.

18. Le Corbusier: *Towards a New Architecture;* translated by Frederick Etchells; New York, Payson & Clarke, Ltd., 1927.

19. —— *The City of To-morrow and Its Planning;* translated by Frederick Etchells; New York, Payson & Clarke, Ltd., 1927.

20. *Le Corbusier and Pierre Jeanneret. Ihr gesamtes Werk von 1910-1929;* herausgegeben und übersetzt von O. Stonorov und W. Boesiger; Zürich, Dr. H. Girsberger & Co., 1930.

21. Lethaby, W. R.: *Philip Webb and His Work;* London, Oxford University Press, 1935.

22. Mackail, J. W.: *The Life of William Morris;* London, New York and Bombay, Longmans, Green & Co., 1899, 2 vols.

23. *Erich Mendelsohn. Das Gesamtschaffen des Architekten.* Skizzen, Entwürfe, Bauten. Berlin, Rudolf Mosse, 1930.

24. Moore, Charles: *Daniel H. Burnham;* Boston and New York, Houghton Mifflin Co., 1921, 2 vols.

25. Morrison, Hugh: *Louis Sullivan, Prophet of Modern Architecture;* New York, W. W. Norton & Co., Inc., 1935.

26. Mumford, Lewis: *The Brown Decades;* New York, Harcourt, Brace, 1931.

27. —— *Sticks and Stones;* New York, Boni & Liveright, 1924.

28. Muthesius, Hermann: *Das Englische Haus;* Berlin, E. Wasmuth, A. G. 1908, 3 Bde.

29. Oud, J. J. P.: *Holländische Architektur;* Bauhausbücher Nr. 10; Munich, Albert Langen, 1926.

30. Prévost, Jean: *Eiffel;* Paris, Editions Rieder, 1929.

31. Schinkel, Karl Friedrich: *Karl Friedrich Schinkel: Briefe, Tagebücher, Gedanken;* ausgewählt, eingeleitet und erläutert von Hans Mackowsky. Berlin, Propyläen-Verlag.

32. —— *Aus Schinkel's Nachlass. Reisetagebücher, Briefe und Aphorismen;* mitgeteilt von Alfred Freiherr von Wolzogen. 4 vols. Berlin, R. Decker, 1863.

33. Semper, Gottfried: *Der Stil in den technischen und architektonischen Künsten;* Munich, F. Bruckmann, 1878-79, 2 vols.

34. Sullivan, Louis Henry: *Autobiography of an Idea;* New York, Press of The American Institute of Architects, Inc., 1924.

35. Taut, Bruno: *Die Auflösung der Städte oder Die Erde eine gute Wohnung oder auch: Der Weg zur Alpinen Architektur;* Hagen i. Westf., Folkwang Verlag, 1920.

36. Tuckerman, Henry T.: *A Memorial of Horatio Greenough;* New York, G. P. Putnam & Co., 1853.

37. Vallance, Aymer: *William Morris, His Art, His Writings and His Public Life;* London, G. Bell & Sons, 1909.

38. van de Velde, Henry: *Die Renaissance im modernen Kunstgewerbe,* Berlin, Bruno und Paul Cassirer, 1901.

39. Van Rensselaer, Mrs. Schuyler: *Henry Hobson Richardson and His Works;* Boston and New York, Houghton Mifflin & Co., 1889.

40. Wijdeveld, Henricus Theodorus, ed.: *The Life-work of the American Architect Frank Lloyd Wright;* Sandpoort, Holland, C. A. Mees, 1925.

41. Whitaker, Charles Harris: *Rameses to Rockefeller,* The Story of Architecture; New York, Random House, 1934.

42. Wright, Frank Lloyd: *An Autobiography;* London and New York, Longmans, Green & Co., 1932.

43. Wood, Edith Elmer: *Recent Trends in American Housing;* New York, The Macmillan Company, 1931.

B. *A Selected List of Books on Modern Building in General:*

44. Bertram, Anthony: *The House, a Machine for Living In;* London, A. and C. Black, 1935.

45. Cheney, Sheldon: *The New World Architecture;* New York, Longmans, Green & Co., 1930.

46. Joseph Gantner, ed.: *Neues Bauen in der Welt;* Band I: *Russland* von El Lissitzky; Band II: *Amerika* von Richard J. Neutra; Band III: *Frankreich* von Roger Ginzburger; Vienna, Anton Schroll & Co., 1930.

47. Gropius, Walter: *Bauhausbauten Dessau;* Munich, Albert Langen, 1930.

BIBLIOGRAPHY

48. Gropius, Walter: *The New Architecture and the Bauhaus;* London, Faber & Faber, Ltd., 1935.

49. Hitchcock, Henry Russell, Jr., and Johnson, Philip: *The International Style: Architecture Since 1922;* New York, W. W. Norton, 1932.

50. —— *Modern Architecture; Catalogue of the International Exhibition;* New York, Museum of Modern Art, 1932.

51. Holme, C. G., ed.: *Industrial Architecture;* Introduction by L. H. Bucknell; London, The Studio Ltd., 1935.

52. Malkiel-Jirmounsky, M.: *Les tendances de l'architecture contemporaire;* Paris, Libraire Delagrave, 1930.

53. Mendelsohn, Erich: *Neues Haus, Neue Welt;* Berlin, R. Mosse, 1932.

54. Pevsner, Nikolaus: *Pioneers of the Modern Movement From William Morris to Walter Gropius;* London, Faber & Faber, 1936.

55. Platz, Gustav Adolf: *Die Baukunst der Neuesten Zeit;* Berlin, Propyläen-Verlag, 1927.

56. Sartoris, Alberto: *Gli elementi dell' architettura funzionale;* Milan, U. Hoepli, 1935.

57. Sullivan, Louis: *Kindergarten Chats,* edited by Claude F. Bragdon; Lawrence, Kansas, Scarab Fraternity Press, 1934.

58. Taut, Bruno: *Modern Architecture;* London, The Studio Ltd., 1929.

59. Towndrow, Frederic: *Architecture in the Balance;* New York, Frederick A. Stokes & Co., 1936.

60. Vischer, Julius, and Hilbersheimer, Ludwig: *Beton als Gestalter;* Stuttgart, Julius Hoffmann, 1928.

61. Wright, Frank Lloyd: *Modern Architecture;* Princeton, N. J., Princeton University Press, 1931.

INDEX

231

[57